BEDS AND BORDERS
Traditional and Original Garden Designs

BEDS AND BORDERS
Traditional and Original Garden Designs

WENDY B. MURPHY

PHOTOGRAPHS BY JOANNE AND JERRY PAVIA

FOREWORD BY KEN DRUSE

Houghton Mifflin Company • Boston 1990

A RUNNING HEADS BOOK

Published in the United States by
Houghton Mifflin Company
2 Park Street
Boston, MA 02108

BEDS AND BORDERS
was conceived and produced by
Running Heads Incorporated
55 West 21st Street
New York, NY 10010

Editor: Charles de Kay
Designer: Liz Trovato
Production Manager: Linda Winters

All photographs by Joanne and Jerry Pavia
except those on pages 26, 76, 77, and 79, are by
Rosalind Creasy.

Typeset by Crane Typesetting Service, Inc.
Color separations by Hong Kong Scanner Craft
    Co., Ltd.
Printed and bound in Singapore through
    Palace Press, San Francisco

Library of Congress Cataloging in Publication Data
Murphy, Wendy B.
    Beds and borders : traditional and original
garden designs / by Wendy B. Murphy ;
    photographs by Jerry and Joanne Pavia.
        p.   cm.
    Includes bibliographical references.
    ISBN 0-395-51759-1
    1. Landscape gardening.   2. Raised bed
gardening.   3. Garden borders.   4. Gardens—
Design.   I. Pavia, Jerry.   II. Pavia, Joanne.
III. Title.
SB473.M86   1990
716—dc20   90-4341
                                             CIP

0 9 8 7 6 5 4 3 2 1

BOMC offers recordings and compact discs, cassettes
and records. For information and catalog write to
BOMR, Camp Hill, PA 17012.

This book is dedicated to my mother, Camilla Buehr. A perennial flower.

Contents

Foreword by Ken Druse 8

Author's Preface 12

CHAPTER **1:**

Bed and Border Basics

22

Practical Planning 24
Planning the Floral
  Picture 30
The Formal Style 35
The Informal Style 38
Edgings 41
Plant Selection 42
Color Scheming 45
Color Strategy 48
Planting by Height 50
Maintaining a Fresh
  Appearance 52
Garden Styles from the
  Formal to the Natural 54

CHAPTER **2:** Themes and Variations   58

Bed Shapes   60
A Selection of Borders   67
By the Water   72
Edible Beds   76
Urban Beds and Borders   80
Rock Gardens   84
Herbal Gardens   90
The Wild Look   94

Green Gardens   101
Centerpieces   106
Old-Fashioned Beds   110
Woodland Gardens   114
Raised Beds and Borders   118
Terraced Beds   126
Formal Beds and Borders   130
The Dry Garden   135

CHAPTER **3:** Hortus Prospectus   138

Acknowledgments   155

Index   156

Foreword

After your property has settled down to its cover of lawn, trees and shrubs, you might feel something is still missing. After all, a house doesn't become a home until the heart of a family beats within it. What separates a backyard from a garden? The plantings are the heart of the landscape. Their warmth and color are irresistible. The garden bed or border extols the always-changing beauty of nature as drifts of one color turn into waves of another. Just as a patio adds outdoor living space, the bed or border completes the successful horticultural environment. It's one of the first things that every gardener wants to create. But where to begin? How do you plan and plant your first garden bed or border?

When you think of the typical border, you may think first of the massive perennial plantings popularized just before the turn of the century by the British garden designer Gertrude Jekyll. You'd be hard-pressed to create something as large as these bygone borders, which were often ten to twenty feet deep and one to two hundred feet long. Even if you have the property to support such a creation, it's unlikely that you could enlist an army of well-trained helpers to maintain it. Your flower garden does not have to be as grand in scale as Miss Jekyll's, but it can still give you as much pleasure: bigger isn't necessarily better. You can make substantial borders of flowers in shades of mauve, blue, and white, for example, or just a small island planting filled with a happy blend of blooming specimens.

In fact, beds and borders, no matter what their size, offer a marvelous range of opportunity for self-expression. The possibilities are limited only by the climate and the gardener's imagination. Consider formal geometric flower beds, cool green foliage gardens, or charming borders of woodland wildflowers. A small pool or pond can take the place of a bed as it becomes a site for waterlilies and other aquatic plants. Beds and borders of edible plants can be designed with the plants' ornamental qualities in mind.

Whatever direction you take, the goal in creating a bed or border is not only to experience the passion of collecting colorful plants but to plan for as much visual interest as possible in the particular landscape. A bed or border exists in a four-dimensional world. There is the artistic challenge of arranging the line and plane of design and the form and texture of foliage and flowers. But there is also season-long color to consider: time is the fourth dimension of the garden bed or border. And planning for blossoms (or harvests) in succession is the essence of the medium.

Reading *Beds and Borders* is the perfect first step in designing the consummate beds and borders for your garden. This book is a complete introduction to these fantastic landscape inventions. Throughout its pages, you'll find ideas for schemes and plantings that will not only inspire you but offer you insight and plenty of solid information on how to achieve the results you desire. The photographs reveal the careful association of foliage and the tasteful combinations of colors that convey the easy elegance and stylish control of a well-executed bed or border. This book will open the gate to your garden ideal.

Ken Druse is the author of *The Natural Garden* and garden editor of *House Beautiful*.

BEDS AND BORDERS
Traditional and Original Garden Designs

Author's Preface

"What rarer object can there be on earth, (the motions of the Celestial bodies except) than a beautiful and Odoriferous Garden plot Artificially composed. . . ." Thomas Hyll, The Gardeners Labyrinth *(1577).*

Ever since early civilizations, we have been easily seduced by the glories of a well-tended garden. Then, as now, gardens were Nature perfected, a kind of paradise on earth, where the lessons of God's great hand were writ small enough for mortals to read and understand. But until rather recently, the enjoyment of gardens has been a luxury limited chiefly to the privileged classes, the only people in a position to commit the necessary labor (needless to say, hired labor) and the necessary land and expense to such involving enterprises.

Over the centuries, just what society has deemed to be perfection or even merely beauty in gardens has been subject to many shifts in taste and much impassioned, not to say dogmatic, argument. In some centuries, the arbiters of fashion have found acceptable only those arrangements of plants that were formal, symmetrical, and on a grand scale, as though man's ability to tame everything on earth was somehow sublime. In other periods, the test of beauty has turned upon the garden's imitation of the native wilds, or its display of colors for color's sake, or its reliance on exotic and rare specimens to the exclusion of many beautiful domestic species. In the process, the gardens of one era have repeatedly been plowed under to make way

Caught on the brink of springtime perfection, this handsome member of the primrose family, Himalayan primrose (Primula denticulata), *is about to unfold its sweet-scented clusters of lilac-like blossoms.*

With brilliant bursts of color against a lush background of greens, this informal border, right, can scarcely contain its floral beauty.

for the ideas or ideals of another. Much that was wonderful aesthetically was all but forgotten, and not a few fine plants were cast aside to make way for "progress."

Fortunately, all these narrowly focused approaches to gardening have faded along with the kind of aristocratic society that so long sustained them. In our more democratic times, gardeners feel free at last to borrow from many times and places or to be inventive in their own ways. And the gardens they create, though typically on a far smaller scale than in times past, exhibit a greater diversity of plant materials, floral and foliage colors, and garden layout than has before been possible.

In this book we will demonstrate this happy fact with a dazzling selection of contemporary North American gardens, some of them public but many more of them in private hands. Our focus will be on beds and borders, those special areas of annual and perennial planting that are the heart and soul of any garden. In terminology we will follow professional usage, reserving the term "bed" for any planting area that is meant to be seen freely on all sides, such as the traditional knot garden surrounded by lawn; and "border" for any plot along the margins of a lawn or path, the side of a building, the edge of a pond, or some other substantial and permanent feature in the landscape.

We begin with a chapter on "Bed and Border Basics," setting forth the historical and practical considerations in laying out and planting beds and borders—how to orient them to create near views and far vistas, how to determine their most congenial dimensions, and how to select among the many choices in formal and informal shapes. We will also talk about some of the clever ways

The interplay of tall and short forms, spiky and round flowers, smooth and shiny foliage, and lots of pretty colors makes for a border that is thoroughly interesting in spring, summer, and fall.

Drifts of tulips play hide and seek among the permanent plantings of Japanese maple and Alberta spruce. The bulbs are growing through an undergrowth of forget-me-nots.

in which bed and border locations can be used to accent good features in the landscape (and disguise the not-so-good) and show a number of professional techniques for constructing and framing both raised and flat beds and borders. Finally, we will discuss the important issue of color as it relates to flowering plants and foliage, describing ways in which it can be used harmoniously and in contrast, and as accents and "drifts."

Our second chapter, "Themes and Variations," makes a coast-to-coast tour of existing bed and border gardens, showing superb solutions to such special planting situations as a border for a small city plot, a flower bed at waterside, and beds in the Victorian and Japanese traditions. From time to time we will pause to take a closer look at a particularly nice solution to edging, an unusual juxtaposition of colors, a dramatic play of texture against an old stone wall, or an exceptionally skillful interplay of annuals and perennials. We will also share the garden designer's practical reasoning behind his or her work— how the bed or border relates to the surrounding landscape and house, how sun and wind exposure, soil and moisture conditions, have influenced choices in plants. And we will pass along the experts' tips on how to plant and maintain various types of gardens for maximum beauty and vigor throughout the season and over the years.

Last, in the chapter "Hortus Prospectus," we profile in useful detail more than sixty species and varieties of flowering and foliage plants, herbs, bulbs, and low-growth shrubs that are ideally suited to growing in beds and borders. Everything you need to know about hardiness, color, foliage, height, habit, time and length of bloom, propagation, ongoing care, and companionable plantings is included. And for those readers with an interest in horticultural history, the chapter also offers glimpses into the origin and popularity of the examples given, some of which have claimed a place in English cottage gardens for centuries; others are very recent additions to the gardener's palette, dating from the late nineteenth century.

We hope that, armed with all this vital information, you will be inspired to experiment anew in your own garden, choosing from among the scores of good ideas in these pages and picturing those concepts that are particularly applicable to your own situation and your own ambition.

Yellow calceolaria and pink-to-purple verbena make unusual partners in a bed of annuals. They combine in a color combination typical of the Victorian era, when this type of border treatment was all the rage.

In this verdant garden, the color green is shown in all its lush, mysterious possibilities. The sandy path winds between plantings of ferns and azaleas.

Among the best known and best loved of garden plants, the genus Iris *offers some 150 species that rank as stand-out performers in the June garden. Shown opposite are fibrous-rooted Siberian iris, which are among the hardiest and easiest to grow of all the iris clan.*

In a lovely example of analogous color scheming, pale pink poppies, violet and purple painted daisies, and lavender-tinted meadow rue grow together, above, with the graceful white spires of bugbane for an early summer display.

A close-up of the California poppies (Eschscholzia californica) in the terraced bed, opposite, shows how well planned plantings can work with landscaping: the vibrant orange of the flowers beautifully complements the border of edging brick.

CHAPTER

1 Bed and Border Basics

Yellow-cupped sundrops make a tallish ground cover. Each bloom lasts only a day, but because plants spread quickly, forming dense clumps that send up new blooms from June to August, they are fine border perennials.

In this skillfully designed bed, opposite, plants of many different forms, heights, foliage textures and colors, and, most of all, flower colors, come together harmoniously. The towering presence at back is globe thistle (Echinops).

A bed or border, when well designed and lovingly cared for, is a unique reflection of the taste, intelligence, and personality of its creator. Designing such a work of art requires planning, organization, and a good measure of patience. Good things don't happen overnight, and great things don't happen in a season.

We'll get to the planning and organization in a moment, but first let's talk about attitude. In the pages that follow, you will come upon scores of beds and borders that could make a body green with envy. You may think such artistry so far beyond you that there's no point in even trying. But you are missing the point. Gardening, as England's William Robinson has said, "is an inexhaustible art." It offers pleasures at every level of expertise and is never finished. By studying the ways in which others have used the elements of gardening to advantage, you can begin to formulate your own personal approach. Then, starting small and keeping your first essays simple, you can produce a bed or border that is eminently satisfying and attractive. And the first year's rewards will give you courage to go on and on, experimenting, refining, growing as a garden artist.

A good place to begin your gardening odyssey is, literally, right in your own backyard with an examination of your garden's physical situation, its siting, soil conditions, and climate.

Practical Planning

Siting: The farmer naturally strives to site his vegetable patch or orchard in the very best place his land affords, but in locating an ornamental garden you rarely have that much freedom. Chances are, your beds and borders have to fit within an existing scheme in which a house, a driveway, a terrace, paths and walkways, trees, hedges, and a host of other givens have already grabbed off some of the choicest territory. Perhaps the property has some physical shortcomings that you want to disguise, or a feature in the distant landscape that you want to draw attention to. In addition, you have aesthetic considerations to address. What remains in terms of potential sites may not have the ideal sun exposure, the best soil, or the most interesting natural features as background, but such challenges should not be discouraging. They simply mean that you may have to look for more imaginative solutions in the bed and border designs you devise.

With this proviso, however, it must be said that ample sunshine, coupled with adequate air circulation, shelter from excessive wind, and well-drained fertile soil are the most desirable features to look for in siting any garden. How much of each may be needed for optimum success depends upon the particular plant materials you ultimately choose to grow. If, for example, you have your heart set on growing any of the flowering plants that require full sun three to six hours a day—and that describes the great majority of herbaceous perennials—then you should not plant them in a border on the north side of a two-story house where the summer sun never shines. The result is almost certain to be leggy, spindly growth with few or no blossoms for your trouble. Find another location for your sun-worshippers and use the northern location for a bed of azaleas, rhododen-

dron, and shortias.

The best sites in terms of air circulation are neither too exposed nor too sheltered. Tall, extravagantly headed, thin-stemmed flowers, in particular, do not tolerate strong winds, which can knock them flat right at the moment of their greatest triumph. And even shorter plants can be stunted in development if they have to struggle unprotected on a hilltop or along a coastal shoreline. Plants growing too close to a wall or in the hot, stagnant lee of the land can suffer in a different way, falling prey to plant diseases that tend to prosper in such conditions. If you cannot avoid these extremes, you may have to forgo some of the more sensitive species in favor of plants distinguished for their ability to cope under adverse conditions.

All things considered, the most environ-

For an island bed, opposite, two species of stonecrop—tallish **Sedum reflexum** and lower-growing **Sedum spurium**—have been planted in interlocking triangles.

Difficult terrain has been turned to advantage in this alpine rock garden, above. The occasional bursts of color from cottage pinks (Dianthus) strike high notes.

Tidy lettuce plants make good neighbors for gorgeous Iceland poppies. Interplanting flowers and edibles dates back to early English cottage gardens.

mentally attractive site for a border will always be facing due south (or due north if your garden is in the Southern Hemisphere!) with a high, sheltering wall, hedge, or other sort of windbreak at its back, but not so close as to crowd. Siting an island bed is generally simpler in practical terms; by dint of being out in the lawn, it is virtually assured good sun exposure and air circulation, though depending on the terrain and prevailing breezes it may still have wind to worry about.

Soil Conditions: Soil has three layers, but it is generally only the uppermost layer, the 6 to 8 inches of topsoil, that concern the bed and border maker. By contrast, subsoil also matters when planting larger shrubs and trees.

To evaluate your topsoil's condition, you look chiefly at its structure, chemistry, and fertility. All of these factors are amenable to improvement, but any changes should be made now, while you are still in the planning stages, well before the first plant is set in the ground. This will allow these changes you make to become integral to the growing medium, and it will also give existing perennial weeds plenty of time to show themselves and, with luck, be banished.

Topsoil comes in three basic types, sandy soil, clay, and loam. If your soil is sandy, its particles are relatively coarse, which means that roots have an easy time penetrating, but sandy soil also lacks moisture-retentive capabilities and probably organic materials as well. If your soil has a high component of clay, its particles are rather fine and are inclined to stick together, to compact excessively when wet, and to drain poorly, all of which make underground growth difficult if not impossible for fragile-rooted plants. If your soil is of the loamy sort, it will be midway between sand and clay in texture, and probably darker in color. Chances are, it will also have a good number of juicy earthworms in residence.

Anyone who starts with loam is lucky indeed, for such soil tends to hold just enough moisture and air to keep plants vigorous in all but drought conditions, accommodates new root growth well, and has its own built-in supply of microorganisms and nutrients to keep it alive and active. Sandy and clay soils, on the other hand, will need balancing and improving to sustain a garden. To amend sandy soil, dig in peat moss for moisture retention and rotted compost, well-aged manure, or other organic materials for nutrients. To upgrade clay soil, add sand for better drainage and organic materials for greater fertility. And if your soil seems beyond redemption—all "hard-pan" subsoil and construction rubble—you might consider building raised beds or borders using an 8-inch layer of imported loam over the existing soil.

Your soil's chemistry is a measure of its level of acidity or alkalinity, as graded on a pH scale of 1 to 15. The majority of perennials prefer a pH in the neutral (7.0) to slightly acid (6.0) range; woodland plants naturally favor a moderately acid soil closer to 5.0 pH. So after you have determined your plant selections but before you put any of them in the ground, you ought to make your own soil test with one of those inexpensive kits available at garden centers. If your soil reads too acid, apply lime at a rate of 3–4 pounds per 100 square feet, water it in deeply, and test again in a few days. If your pH comes in as too alkaline ("sweet") for your purposes, correct with ammonium sulfate or iron sulfate as directed, or apply an acid-type fertilizer, water, and test again in a few days.

While we are on the subject of fertilizers and fertility, remember that though soil naturally comes with a certain amount of nitrogen, phosphorus, potassium, and trace minerals, and the addition of structure-im-

Ornamental grasses are coming into their own as elements of beds and borders. Blue oat grass (Helictotrichon sempervirens) *and 'Dark Delight' New Zealand flax* (Phormium) *provide interest in a California garden.*

The simplest of plantings—hosta and columbine meadow rue—combine to create a low-key divider between the lawn and the wilder salt marshes beyond. Color is kept at a minimum to avoid competing with the fine views.

proving organic materials adds more, many plants are voracious feeders, capable of depleting the soil in a matter of weeks. Part of routine maintenance once you have your plants established will be to top dress them periodically with organic or synthetic fertilizers; it's also a good idea to introduce a baseline supply of nutrients at the outset so that they will be available several inches down when needed. This is especially true in beds and borders destined to hold permanently residing perennials. The simplest measure is to add a so-called complete fertilizer at a rate of 2–4 pounds per 100 square feet as you are digging the bed. For most flowering perennials and annuals the formula of choice is 10–10–10, which translates as 10% nitrogen, 10% phosphorus, and 10% potassium.

Climate: Ornamental plants derive much of their wonderful diversity from the fact that they evolved in so many different climatic conditions in so many different parts of the world. And while plant breeders have made it possible for varieties and cultivars to be introduced far beyond the natural range, it is still true that most ornamentals retain within a few degrees the temperature hardiness of their ancestors. So when planning your garden, you should select plants with regard to their suitability to your "hardiness zone" and rainfall patterns. If you are unsure of these details, check with your local garden center. Later, as you come to know your garden more intimately, you may be able to amend zone information with your own observations of the "microclimate," which reflects the site's precise location deep in a valley, in the shelter of a mountain, in the path of moderating ocean breezes, and other ground-level local influences.

Planning the Floral Picture

Though a good border ought to appear art-less, its design should in fact be guided by the same principles that direct the mind and eye in any other art form: balance, rhythm, accent, and harmony.

Balance in garden design is the illusion of stability or equilibrium which comes from massing plant materials of equal weight on either side of some fulcrum, be it in the literal center of the yard or off to one side. *Rhythm* relates to the spatial pattern of "beats" that an arrangement of plants creates for the sake of movement and interest: a sequence of short plants punctuated by a plant of taller habit, a sequence of mound-shaped plants followed by a columnar one, a run of darks with a change-up of light, and so on. *Accents* provide points of excitement within the composition—a brilliant color, a showy plant form—to lead the eye forward. *Harmony* is the unity and completeness of the design, first as it relates to the garden, and second as it relates to the architectural character of its immediate surroundings. In a harmonious composition all the parts must be compatible with the overall mood of the place.

These principles of balance, rhythm, accent, and harmony are of human invention, based on long-established, manmade aesthetic judgments that are always evolving and changing. Unchanging, however, are the physical elements of design, which include form, line, color, and texture. *Form* involves the shape and structure of three-dimensional objects in the garden, ranging from the contours of the ground itself to the shape of beds and borders and the materials that edge them to the habit or shape of the plant materials themselves. In the garden, line is found in the edges of walls and paths, in the boundaries between different surface materials such as grass, earth, and water, and in the silhou-

Mass plantings of cannas and marigolds offer a glowing combination of warm colors for formal bedding schemes. Both species are tender and must await the last frost before being transplanted.

The cheery colors of tuberous begonias, heliotrope, and lobelia provide a bright welcome near a doorway. Red and pink wax begonias complete the picture. In addition, heliotrope's delicious fragrance, reminiscent of cherries, adds an extra sensory pleasure.

ettes of such three-dimensional objects as buildings, trees, rocks, and hedges. Capable of leading the eye into the distance, around a corner, or to an object selected for focal interest, line can be used to tie disparate elements together in a composition. *Color* includes not only the basic colors of buds and flowers, but the subtle ranges of greens and greys of garden foliage, the reds and browns of earth and stems and bark; in all but foliage gardens it is a changing feature, waxing and waning with the seasons. *Texture* relates to the visual appearance of surfaces, from smooth and shiny to rough and spiny, as well as the form and density of foliage and flowers.

Orchestrating a garden design that takes all these aesthetic principles and elements into account is not as difficult as it may sound if you take the parts step by step and work out your plans on paper first. Using a long-distance tape measure (50'–100' is recom-

mended), measure off existing walls, hedges, paths, and other permanent features, such as large trees, in the area where you plan to lay out your borders and beds. Transfer each piece of information in scale to a sheet of graph paper, which will become the basic blueprint for later plant selections.

Now you are ready to address the question of style. Style can be defined as a distinct and consistent way of using balance, rhythm, accent, and harmony to achieve a predetermined "look." Though history has given us dozens of stylistic traditions upon which to draw for inspiration—the Italian Style, the French Style, the Japanese Style, the Cottage Style, the Knot Garden Style (see box)—they all relate in greater or lesser degree to either the formal or the natural school of design. Your choice will properly depend upon the character and ambience of your house and grounds and how you like to live in them.

"Nature's way" could be the theme of this garden bed. The owner, an avid collector of plants, is particularly interested in species distinguished for their long blooming season and handsome foliage. This bed shows off some of her prized rhododendron and azaleas.

The Formal Style

The hallmarks of the formal style are symmetry and elegance, so formal beds and borders are logical choices for houses of like architectural character. In America, that includes houses built in the Classic Revival, Beaux Arts, and Late Victorian styles. Less obvious but equally appropriate pairings are formal gardens with many geometrical houses of contemporary modern design, and formal gardens with urban townhouses.

Formal borders are usually rectangular in shape and take their line from nearby garden features, such as the edge of a rectangular lawn, a straight hedge or path, a driveway, the edge of a patio or terrace, a wall of the house, or its central axis as determined by the front or rear entrance. Often the formal border comes in pairs that are designed to be the mirror image of each other, space for space and plant for plant, so that they hold the entire garden area in a kind of perfect visual balance. A distinct color or texture, or a particular pattern of planting, is often repeated at measured intervals throughout the borders as a unifying device. And contrast is kept at a restrained level. Laid out to best effect on reasonably level ground, with no interruptions such as boulders or trees in the way, the formal border makes for an outdoor room that is calm, classic, and generally very restful.

Low hedges of boxwood and neatly defined rectilinear paths give these beds a formal framework and keep them looking tidy and attractive even during the months when the perennials die back.

Border size is mostly a matter of taste and convenience, though a formal border should not be so small or large as to seem out of scale with the rest of the garden room or the kinds of plants to be placed there. The width ought to be sufficient to accommodate several ranks of plants, but not so wide as to make weeding and working from the outside impractical. Most professionals recommend borders from 4 to 5 feet wide with a narrow service path at the back, where it is out of sight. If something wider is called for, then a concealed passageway running lengthwise through the center is virtually a must for weeding and working. Use your original site plan as the basic blueprint, and work out the details on an overlay of tracing paper. Transfer the measurements directly to the area to be planted, set stakes in the ground to mark the edges, and run string around the perimeter. Then step back to confirm that everything checks out visually to your satisfaction.

Formal island beds, which are nearly identical in spirit to borders, are also characterized by their geometric shapes—the circle, oval, hexagon, square, or rectangle. They should also be located with an eye to balanced composition, which conventionally means somewhere out on the lawn equidistant between two other major garden elements such as matched borders. A note of caution: An island bed inevitably draws the eye to more distant perspectives beyond; if the distant scene is one that enhances the character of the garden and grounds, this is all to the good, but if the far side is not precisely of your choosing, then the island bed might run counter to your purposes.

Finding the right proportions for an island bed also requires care. A classic rule of thumb that still bears following is: Select the most prominent location from which the bed is going to be viewed, typically a central doorway, or the center of a terrace or patio, and measure the distance to the bed's location. Make the width of the bed a little less than half of the distance calculated. Thus, in a good-sized garden in which the island bed is to be 40 feet from the patio, a suitable planting area might be 16 to 19 feet across. The depth ought to be at least twice the height of the tallest perennial plants you will be using, which is to say 10 feet if your tallest plants are to be 5 feet tall.

Elegance is achieved in the meticulous care with which the formal border and bed are maintained, from the regimental precision with which plants are set in the ground to the almost daily excising of weeds and manicuring of edges. Also essential to their glorious effects are the kinds of plant materials selected: neat, firm plants of uniform color and disciplined habit, characteristics which we will examine more closely in Chapter 3, where we explore some of the outstanding perennials and annuals available today.

Flat formal beds can be given a third dimension with the addition of plant-filled vases, urns, or strawberry jars, as in this courtyard garden.

The Informal Style

In a small, irregular space such as this urban backyard, an informal layout is often the most effective solution. Here different paving materials link separate planting areas, defining edges in the bargain.

The informal border, by contrast, is most assuredly asymmetric in shape, more than willing to wander, and given to plants whose habits can be exuberant, unruly, or idiosyncratic. Informal borders are also far more adaptable to their immediate surroundings; they can turn corners comfortably, skirt large boulders and ponds, rise and fall with the terrain, and dart beneath the shady shelter of an existing tree. This does not mean, however, that the informal border is formless and without its own set of rules; it simply finds its organization in more subtle elements. For example, balance in the informal border can be won by playing color against color, or light against dark.

Plants in informal beds are usually allowed to grow to their natural shapes, rather than being manicured into neat little globes or boxes. Different kinds of plants tumble together in happy profusion. One point to keep in mind as you mix and match plants, though, is to make sure you plant several of each type. Even in informal gardens, start with just a few different kinds of plants and plant several of each type. A bed containing one each of thirty different plants will look haphazard rather than informal.

In determining the shape and size of the informal border and island bed, apply the same practical standards as you would for formal planting areas: Make them neither too small nor too large for the scale of the area, and always leave some convenient means of getting at the interior when performing maintenance chores. An easy way to work out the most pleasing shape of your intended bed or border is to describe it on the ground with a length of flexible garden hose; keep rearranging the hose—changing curves, enlarging and diminishing the area—until you are satisfied with what you see.

*The informal mood of this desert garden suits
the relaxed feelings of the Southwest. The large
opuntias form the backbone of the garden, with
rosy purple verbena and other flowering plants
drifting around their feet. Scatterings of river-
washed stone have been introduced as an
attractive source of textural relief.*

Edging materials like these reproduction Victorian tiles, above, provide a tidy barrier between border and path or lawn. They discourage vigorous plants from running amok, though some periodic trimming is always necessary.

Brick edging draws the line between a semi-formal bed and the vigorous lawn beyond it, opposite. The earth tone of the brick also sets off the delicate colors of grey-green lamb's ears and purple catmint planted within.

Edgings

Edgings frame the floral painting, set the front off from the surrounding lawn, path, or driveway, and provide the contrast of a different texture. Properly installed, edgings also discourage lawn grass and weeds from sending subsurface roots into the planting area and hold back perennials given to trespassing on the lawn. Many weatherproof materials work well. Some are decorative in their own right, some quite invisible when installed, so the choice really hinges on where the bed or border is located and what is most in keeping with its overall design.

Formal borders that front on paved paths are automatically set off from the immediate surroundings. But where they adjoin gravel paths they need an upright edging that rises high enough to contain the pebbles and sinks its feet 3 to 4 inches to remain stable and check underground grass runners. One such material is terra-cotta edging tile, which is manufactured in a variety of traditional Victorian designs including a rope pattern, curved, and diamond-pointed tops, all available in well-stocked garden supply stores.

Edging tiles are also suitable for formal borders and beds that front on lawns, though the grass will always need to be trimmed by hand or with a string trimmer for a neat appearance (mowers cannot come close enough to do the job). More convenient in the lawn situation are aged brick, tiles, and cut stone set crossways and horizontally at ground level. The edge they make is 8 to 12 inches wide (a standard brick is 8 inches long), which is wide enough to run the mower up close without injuring plants in the front row.

For a somewhat softer looking formal edge, use low-growing boxwood or other dwarf evergreens to form a continuous straight line, but be prepared to hand clip from time to time to maintain their traditional geometric

trim. Sweet herbs such as marjoram, savory, thyme, and lavender are other edging choices that are particularly suited to herb and knot gardens, where they have been used for hundreds of years.

For a still softer edge, suitable for either formal or informal situations, you can run the mulched soil right up against a well-tended line of grass. To keep the twain from meeting, however, you will need to true up the edges in spring and fall with a turf edger or spade and hand trim them frequently during the growing season. A nearly invisible 4- to 6-inch barrier strip of metal or plastic, set in along the line where border and lawn meet, with perhaps 1 inch protruding at the top, keeps these green neighbors from mingling.

Handsome field stones and rough-cut stones are other good choices for an informal border, particularly a woodland garden planted with shade-loving alpine plants and other dwarf shrubs. Pressure-treated wood timbers and railroad ties work fine in informal angular beds but are not suitable where curving forms are called for.

Plant Selection

A horticultural lexicon of plant shapes—from the bold, exotic, bayonet-shaped leaves of the yucca to the diminutive, fragile growth of alyssum—makes this desert garden interesting to explore visually.

Although herbaceous perennials have had their aesthetic ups and downs in aristocratic gardens, they have always been the heart of the typical American home flower garden as well as the English cottage garden. The reasons are obvious: Their hardiness, ease of culture, floral beauty, and extraordinary range of colors, heights, textures, and blooming times make them unbeatable choices for the low-maintenance garden. In planning your garden, then, it makes good sense to begin your plant selections with these long-lived stalwarts (unless you are specifically recreating a Victorian carpet bed of tender annuals). To get to know just how rich your choices are, study the selections that appear throughout this volume, and read in particular pages 138–153, where perennials of particular distinction are described in detail. There are, in fact, hundreds of cultivars and varieties available and more being added all the time. To get a sense of what your options really are, develop the habit of browsing through the offerings of your local gardening center in season, reading mail order catalogues, and keeping a notebook of plant names and sources that you collect from friends and acquaintances. The plant sales departments of botanical gardens and historical restorations are also very good places to look.

Many gardeners are happy to devote their beds and borders exclusively to herbaceous perennials, but for the longest possible flowering season—from early spring to late fall —a "mixed border" is a more satisfying route to travel. The mixed border typically contains spring-flowering bulbs of various sorts, including tulips, fritillaria, and daffodils and other narcissi; an assortment of summer and fall annuals that fill the gaps created by the die-back of some perennials; and perhaps some ornamental grasses and evergreens.

In designing a period bed, plant selections are best made from among species favored at the time. In this Victorian-style bed, forget-me-nots, pansies, wallflowers, and purple rock cress are all authentic choices.

*Of all the color schemes available, polychrome certainly offers the widest latitude in plant
selections. And sometimes it leads to happy surprises, as in the conjunction of orange azaleas and tulips.*

Color Scheming

Many a new gardener falls head over heels in love with color in choosing plants for his first beds and borders only to be disappointed when the floral fireworks were supposed to begin. The flowers that were going to be wonderful together turn out to look pallid or uninteresting side by side; or, worse yet, they clash unattractively, cancel each other out visually, or flower at sufficiently different times to have no effect at all on each other. It's a hard lesson to learn after putting in so much work. Better to do some homework about the nature of color beforehand, determine for yourself what kind of overall color effect will really serve your purposes most effectively, and then go after it systematically, choosing that combination and concentration of plant varieties that can carry it off as a continuous display.

The way colors interrelate optically is determined largely by their position in the color spectrum, visible in nature in the rainbow and often represented on paper in the artist's color wheel. Within the spectrum red, yellow, and blue are designated as primary colors, and orange, green, and violet are their immediate derivatives, each one a 50–50 mix of a neighboring pair of primaries. Colors that are related by shared pigments tend to be harmonious; colors that have no common color thread are said to be in contrast. Colors also have "temperature." Reds, oranges, and yellows are perceived as warm; blues and greens are experienced as cool.

When it comes to garden flowers, pure spectral hues are rarely to be found; most colors in nature have some pigment from a neighboring hue, and are tempered further by one of the other dimensions of color, such as its value (the degree of lightness or darkness, tints and shades) and its intensity (the degree of saturation, which is to say bright-

ness or dullness). A flower's texture and shape also influence its apparent color—the lemon yellow of the yellow loosestrife is never going to appear as intense as the lemon yellow of the tulip because of the difference in their flower forms, the first small, delicate, and almost transparent, the second large, opaque, with densely enfolded matte petals.

The various ways of combining some or all of these colors intentionally are called color schemes, and these really come down to four systems. None of the systems can be said to be intrinsically "better" than any other, though from a personal standpoint every gardener is sure to have a favorite scheme with one or

The complementary combinations of yellow and violet and of red and green make for visual effects that work best when blended in drifts.

more of his or her favorite colors used in it.

The most controlled approach to color in the garden is the *monochromatic* scheme, which marshalls only those plants with flowers in various tints and shades of one color. Perhaps the most famous example of the monochromatic scheme is the elegant garden of white-flowering roses, iris, lilacs, and lilies at Sissinghurst Castle, Kent, England, devised in the 1930's by Vita Sackville-West and her husband, Sir Harold Nicolson. The all-one-color scheme is certainly not for everyone or every situation, for it is both formal in its appearance and requires a kind of disciplined plant selection that few of us would willingly undertake. (At Sissinghurst there are many gardens, so having an all-white garden was certainly not a case of doing without color altogether.) A variation on the one-color garden is the seasonally monochromatic, in which a single color dominates in spring, after which a second color takes sole proprietorship in summer, and a third color group of flowers comes on to celebrate fall. The trick here, of course, is to see that each dominant color departs on schedule before the next appears, even if it means pruning out straggler blossoms during transitions. Monochromatic schemes often have a cool and restful effect.

A second color scheme combines colors that are opposites on the painter's color wheel: yellow with violet, red with green, orange with blue. These *complementary* combinations, which usually depend on really bright-hued flowers, are vivid, even aggressive, in the ways they seize the viewer's attention. Depending on one's taste, complementary colors can be used at full strength (side by side) or tempered slightly with foliage plants or white flowers planted between the bold primaries. Another way to gentle their effects ever so slightly is to interplant them where they meet so that no hard color edges are perceived at a distance. When one of the warm colors is paired with one of the cool colors,

Sometimes color combinations can be subtle. The yellow centers of the daisies echo the yellow of the ranunculus behind them.

the warm color will appear to be much closer, the cool color to recede.

Analogous color schemes use a limited number of colors that are physical neighbors of one another in the spectrum. Flowers in the yellow, yellow-orange, and orange ranges are said to be analogous, as are blues, blue-violets, purples, and pinks. Analogous schemes are generally easier to use than complementary schemes because they offer an easier, more restful, transition for the eye and tend to be less formal in style.

Undoubtedly the most popular scheme of all is the *polychromatic*, which combines a medley of colors in a gay, even riotous, explosion of hues and tints and shades. Polychrome gardens are reminiscent of the traditional and very informal cottage gardens, and tend to look natural and random in their display. Nonetheless, planning ought to go into the balance, rhythm, and harmony of the parts.

Color Strategy

Once a color scheme has been chosen, the gardener also needs to give careful consideration to how the colors should be distributed. Except for a few notable specimen plants like peonies, most plants take strength only in numbers and only when they are planted in massed groups.

In the mid-nineteenth century the size of groupings and the kinds of plants chosen to effect them were determined solely by their appropriateness to a particular carpet-bed design. Profusely flowering, low-growing annuals were treated as living pigments that filled the blanks of garish paint-by-numbers pictures. Sometimes the colors were massed in rather orderly rows, like stripes in a flag, in which case they were known as "ribbon beds." And sometimes they were used as mere daubs of color patterned to form a floral coat of arms, a set of owner's initials, a pictorial illustration, or some decorative scrollwork pattern. Bedded out from the greenhouse to their appointed bed or border just before their moment of flowering perfection, they were planted in tight little clusters of colors, with any errant blossoms trimmed off to keep them literally picture perfect. The number of colors, and consequently plant varieties, in a bed or border depended strictly upon the complexity of the illustration. Success was

measured by how cunning the artifice.

The antithesis of spotty Victorian color display, and the one most widely favored today, is the "drift" method, first promoted by the influential English painter and garden theorist Gertrude Jekyll at the turn of the century. Jekyll, who did more than anyone else in her day to revive interest in herbaceous perennials, advocated setting the majority of plants in casually shaped serpentine groups as nature might colonize them in a meadow or woodland. Drifts can be laid out so that plants are visually arresting at their flowering peak but relatively recessive before and after. Another advantage of drifts is the way their appearance seems to change as the viewer alters perspective: At one angle the plants are at the front of the border, at another they stand back toward the center, overlapped by one or more forward-ranking drifts whose own colors play against them.

The size of the drift and the number of individual plants needed to fill it will depend upon the flowering profligacy of the plant, the relative robustness or fragility of the blossoms, and the scale of the bed itself, but a mass ought to be sufficient to be seen as a discrete color element from whatever distance it will most often be viewed. For most purposes, a mass averaging about 1 square yard in area is sufficient. If the drifts are made up of herbaceous perennials, it may take two or three growing seasons for the plantings to fill in all the interstices and for their color impact to become fully realized. Resist the impulse to plant for sufficient density in the first year because you will have to divide the perennials almost immediately and risk weakening their stock.

Geraniums and verbenas of rose and similar reddish purple hues join in an analogous scheme that is additionally effective for the different sizes of their blossoms.

The soft yellow of Achillea 'Moonshine' *combines beautifully with violet flowers in complementary color schemes. The look is further softened by the silvery lamb's ears planted in front.*

Planting by Height

The standard rule for borders is: Put the tallest plants toward the back of the garden, the shortest in the front, and the middles in the middle, so that every one of them gets to see and be seen. But if you follow this system too slavishly you will end up with something very artificial looking. Planting in diagonal drifts is a good way around the problem because it inevitably puts some of the lowest plants back toward the second tier, some of the second tier back toward the third, and so on, in a manner that makes the stair-step arrangement less apparent to the eye. Some of the very tall plants at the back of the border may need staking to remain erect, but the stakes will be well covered by the masses of plants in the foreground.

In planting an island bed, which can be seen from all sides, put the tallest plants toward the center, stepping down to lower ones as you approach the edges.

*Ranked by height, this tiny ground-hugging carnation (*Dianthus*), makes a fine edging plant. Similarly, Maltese cross (*Lychnis chalcedonica*), at 30-in. tall, is a natural choice for a mid-border position.*

Four ranks of plants work together effectively in this front-to-rear succession of 10-in. dianthus, 18-in. lavender, 20-in. coreopsis, and 36-in. aconites and delphiniums.

Maintaining a Fresh Appearance

Garden maintenance is a four-season affair, but most of the really hard work is at the beginning, in preparing the soil to receive plants for the first time. Once you are under way, the ongoing tasks are fairly easy, though some are time-consuming. The chores come down to six: weeding, watering, staking, trimming, cleanup in autumn, and periodic dividing.

Weeding is best done on a weekly basis throughout the growing season. The sooner you scotch unwelcome visitors the less trouble they will be, for weeds like nothing better than to take all the water, all the nutrients, and all the rooting space if you let them.

Water as needed. The usual bed or border needs about an inch of water a week, though this will vary somewhat depending on the kinds of plants selected, the absorptive capacity of the soil, the amount and kind of mulch used, and the heat and humidity. (A new, experimental form of water-conserving gardening, called Xeriscaping, needs significantly less; see page 135.) To check conditions in your garden, poke a small hole in the soil to a depth of 1½ inches and see if the earth below that level has any moisture. If it feels dry, it is time to water again. Water thoroughly. A superficial watering that is not sufficient to reach 3 to 4 inches down is worse than nothing, for it encourages thirsty plants to develop shallow roots, making them far less hardy and more susceptible to drought. And water in the morning, preferably before the sun is high in the sky; this gives plant leaves a chance to dry off during the day, important in warding off disease, and minimizes evaporation. Most important, use an efficient water-delivery system, such as a soaker hose placed on the surface of the soil under the mulch early in the season, after the first plant shoots have become visible.

Staking is often necessary for top-heavy plants like peonies and very tall, slender-stalked plants like delphiniums and gaillardias. Set slim green bamboo canes in the ground alongside the stems and anchor the stems invisibly with loosely tied green twists to make a speedy job of it. Or put four or more stakes around the perimeter of a very large plant and connect the stakes with a continuous length of dull-colored twine at a height slightly below the canopy of leaves and flowers. But do not wait until the problem is upon you; stake while the plant is still in the early blossom stage for better results.

Trimming is usually confined to "deadheading" once a week with a pair of snippers in one hand and a trash basket in the other. By getting rid of spent blossoms you not only give the rest of the garden a tidier look but you prevent the over-the-hill plants from putting their remaining energy into seed formation. (Most perennials multiply best through division of their root stock; seeds generally produce inferior plants which, in the case of hybrids, are likely to revert to the characteristics of their unimproved ancestors.) Some perennials also flower for a longer period each year when pruned this way.

Fall cleanup is the last chore of the year, undertaken after the first hard freeze. Faded and dying stalks should be cut down to 3 or 4 inches, and all discarded materials carried away. The remaining stubble is useful for holding down winter mulch—evergreen branches are an attractive as well as a practical choice.

Dividing is the gardener's way of extending the life of perennials while keeping their size and number under control. Not all perennials need this kind of attention, but for the majority that do, the usual frequency is about once every three years. Fall is the best time to divide most perennials unless you live in a climate with extreme winters; in that case the task is better left until spring, when the shocked plants can do their recovering in relatively benign weather. Prune a plant severely before dividing, water the soil around to soften and loosen roots, and then dig the entire plant out, severing as few roots as possible in the process. Divide the plant with a sharp knife if it is fairly small, or take two spading forks, drive them back to back through the center of a larger clump, and press the tops of the handles together to force the tines apart, breaking the root clump in two. After trimming away any damaged or matted materials, return one of the clumps to the enriched hole, taking care to set the crowns at the same level of the soil as they were before dividing; put the other clump in some new location or give it to a friend. Water the divided plant thoroughly to settle the soil around it snugly. Your good efforts now will reward you in the seasons to come.

In this early spring garden, opposite, every plant seems to be at its moment of perfection.

Shearing, dividing, sowing, and replanting keep this bed, above, looking good.

Garden Styles from the Formal to the Natural

The formal style traces its roots to the royal gardens of ancient Egypt. Originating at the edges of the desert, these early palace and temple gardens were artificial oases, whose small, formal, orderly plantings were laid out in long, straight, bedlike rows that paralleled narrow irrigation canals. Generally walled off from the surrounding landscape, the oasis gardens made a virtue out of being distinctly separate from the natural environs. Though many of the details would change over succeeding centuries to accommodate local variations in climate, terrain, and plant life, these first ornamental gardens became the models for the pleasure gardens of Syria, Persia, India, and, ultimately, of imperial Rome. They passed into the Western tradition during the Middle Ages as the four-square cloistered gardens of Christian monasteries and the walled knot gardens and labyrinths of secular castles.

Because the native flowers of Europe were chiefly spring bloomers, and they were all that gardeners had to choose from in those times, gardens were comparatively flowerless for nine or ten months out of twelve, and such horticultural ingenuity as was attempted was mainly with herbs, shrubs, and foliage plants.

With the West's cultural and economic revival during the Renaissance, gardens continued to be laid out in the same orderly and disciplined fashion, only on a scale of magnificence never seen before. In these more peaceful times, the garden's enclosing walls came down to make way for vast parterres, perfectly symmetrical compartments of evergreens, statuary, and fountains laid out on terraces that fell away from the château. Abstractions of gardens, the parterres were not so much meant to be walked in and enjoyed on a personal level as to be seen and admired from

The precision of this planting creates ribbons of color with a formal look.

a distance—better yet, an elevated distance such as the windows of the château's grand salon. Plants were treated as formal architectural elements, to be clipped, snipped, shorn, and shaped to the master plan, and even the surrounding forests were brought under a degree of formal control.

Formalism reached its peak in André Le Nôtre's designs for Versailles in the late seventeenth century and became the standard by which European palaces and country estates were measured for another century or more. Though other styles have since come along with the democratization of gardening, and though few gardens anywhere approach the size of their baroque ancestors, the purely formal style has never gone out of fashion entirely, being practiced in many urban parks as well as in the gardens of historic houses that can still afford the labor-intensive efforts needed to keep them going.

Formal beds and borders can also be found today in private courtyard gardens behind city townhouses, where a formal garden style is most in keeping with the architectural style of the house. The knot garden,

Woodland plants are artfully arranged in this garden which looks both natural and carefully controlled.

too, can still be seen in the backyards of herb gardeners with the time and patience to maintain the low hedges of boxwood or germander that form the pattern of the beds.

About the time that formalism was taking root in the West, its antithesis, naturalism, was developing in China. To the ancient Chinese, gardening was an act of spiritual reverence whose ultimate goal was to represent in symbolic form the sublime order and harmony found in nature itself. Nowhere was man's hand meant to be visible, and nowhere was the line between the garden and the distant landscape sharply drawn; one simply melted into the other in free curves and indistinct lines.

The natural traditions of Chinese gardening exercised a profound influence on other Asian cultures over the centuries, but they remained unknown in the West until the eighteenth century, when pure formalism began to fall out of fashion. Western designers, and most especially English garden designers like Lancelot

"Capability" Brown, then came under the spell of the new Romantic Movement. Vaguely aware of the Oriental tradition of naturalism, and attracted to the idea of imitating nature, they still had no desire to effect the scale and intimacy of the Chinese garden. Rather, they came up with an indigenous style which they called natural but which was really a romanticized, antiqued version of nature. Hills were thrown up and knocked down, streams diverted, woodlands planted in meadows, meadows carved out of former woodlands, and winding carriage roads laid out to replace the promenades and avenues of an earlier, more formal generation. And in case anyone failed to catch the allusions to "Nature Untrammeled," Brown's successors made a point of including all sorts of sentimental fancies in their parklands, from faked Roman ruins to sheep folds, hermit's grottoes, and "wild gardens" as Adam might have found them.

The early–nineteenth-century development of heated glass greenhouses, which coincided with a flood of exotic plant introductions and the invention of the lawnmower, dealt naturalism a temporary setback. Victorian England fell in love with carpet-bedding, the mass planting of greenhouse-raised annuals in intricately patterned beds and borders surrounded by tidy lawns. The finest houses kept scores of gardeners employed in raising and bedding out tens of thousands of tender plants at their moments of perfection. Inevitably, the artifices possible with carpet-bedding reached ridiculous excesses, and in the last quarter of the century William Robinson and Gertrude Jekyll led a return to naturalism. Ironically, their principal inspiration was the homely cottage garden and its sturdy perennials, which had existed for centuries not as a style but as a fact of life among ordinary Englishmen. Robinson's and Jekyll's ideas, and the informal herbaceous perennial border, remain the dominant influences on English and American gardening to this day.

CHAPTER

2 Themes and Variations

In this lush rock garden, rosy red begonias and tiny lavender lobelias take the foreground as the bluish green leaves of bergenia, their tiny clusters of pink flowers already past, continue to add textural counterpoint.

*T*he design and furnishing of a successful flower bed or border are best undertaken as part of an overall scheme of landscaping, with climate, site, architecture, intended use, and your commitment to ongoing maintenance all given careful and due consideration.

On the following pages are examples of some garden beds and borders that have been cleverly tailored to fit just such considerations. They range from formal rose beds and traditional herbal knots to contemporary-looking dry beds that incorporate modern Xeriscaping techniques and plant selections. Enjoy each of these lovely spaces for its unique beauty, of course, but also look to them as sources of new ideas as you make your own gardening plans for the future.

Between the flagstone path and the tall hedge that provides background, this wide border accommodates a glorious diversity of plant forms, shapes, and colors. Particular care has been taken to rank flowering plants by height, with low, sprawling plants like alchemilla in the front, and the tall goatsbeard with its feathery white flower plumes at the rear.

Bed Shapes

Rhythm and movement are essential features in successful landscape design; they are tools by which the garden planner creates designs that have continuing interest and emotional impact. In the tradition of Western landscape design, the dominant elements in creating movement have been the linear shapes of the beds and borders, for these have an immediate and direct impact on the way observers see and experience the garden .

Straight lines, for example, tend to be formal in their effect. They lead the eye quickly from the near ground to the far ground, so that one tends to see neither individual colors nor even individual plants, but a composition that must be taken as a whole. Straight lines have always been a favored choice in the large formal gardens of the past, where huge expanses and carefully chosen vistas were part of the overall scheme, but in today's smaller gardens they should be used with caution, so as not to diminish the sense of space.

Following Zen philosophy, the elements of this Japanese-style garden are designed to represent islands in a pebble sea.

A raised garden has been created within this dramatic zigzag, opposite. The stark sculptural forms echo angular mountains in the distance.

This border is shaped to conform to the old brick
walkway that serves a number of Charleston
townhouses. Bricks set on end trim the border's
edge, their narrow dimensions let them
accommodate the curve nicely.

If you do need to incorporate straight lines in a small garden, such as a straight path running between beds, you can maintain a better sense of space by allowing plants to project slightly into the path at regular intervals to break up the long straight line. If the plants are placed symmetrically and their growth is kept neat, you will still achieve a formal feeling without diminishing the overall feeling of space in the garden.

Curved lines create an atmosphere that is generally more relaxed. The eye is encouraged to move more slowly as it views the bed or border, and to seek "resting places" along the way; this has the overall effect of giving greater play to the particularity of each plant or group of plants. In principle, curved lines are equally congenial with formal and informal beds and borders, though curves that are repeated in some rhythmic fashion are better suited to the formal style, while curves that are asymmetric support the informal style.

Concentric circles tend to create a sense of enclosure and of equilibrium. They are particularly appropriate for a garden room that is meant to be experienced in isolation from other parts of the garden, as in a "secret garden" or a courtyard garden. Like straight lines, they are most often associated with the formal style. The one bed shape that can be said to be purely modern in spirit is the zig-zag, whose lines are bold, exciting, and dynamic.

In choosing any bed shape or border design, it is important to defer to the overall scheme and historical tradition, if any, of the entire garden and to any adjoining structures it must serve and complement.

A horseshoe-shaped bed is used as a kind of architectural device, marking the turning point in an angular terrace. The bed is planted with an outer band of candytuft surrounding a taller interior planting of pansies.

In the Spanish-style courtyard garden, opposite, a bed of evergreen ivy provides textural counterpoint to Spanish patio tile and brilliant white adobe walls, while the rounded corners complement the courtyard's arched entryway.

To complement the roundness of this small central bed, above, the surrounding brick pavement and the shallow rises in terrain in the background have also been set in a circular pattern.

A Selection of Borders

Much of what contemporary gardeners know and believe about good bed and border design can be traced to Gertrude Jekyll, the late–nineteenth-century English visionary who all but invented the herbaceous perennial border as we know it. Jekyll, a one-time landscape painter, compared her work to "painting a picture—a picture hundreds of feet or yards instead of so many inches, painted with living flowers seen by open daylight." She urged gardeners to place the colors "with careful forethought and deliberation, as a painter employs them on his picture, and not dropped in lifeless dabs."

Jekyll was also among the first to come to grips with the fourth dimension, or time, in planning plant selections and locations for her permanent garden. Up until her day, any plan that called for continuity of color through the spring, summer, and fall was almost always realized artificially through the labor-intensive means known as bedding out,

Informal borders face each other across a serpentine flagstone path, opposite. The drifted plantings on the left are chiefly multicolored pansies and snapdragons; those on the right are sweet alyssum and marigolds. All four have been raised from seeds and bedded out after the spring bulbs have gone by.

One of the few remaining examples of large-scale bedding out still practiced in the United States, these public gardens, above, in Manito Park, Spokane, Washington, consist of 90 flower beds marshaling over 10,000 annuals yearly. Here a collection of sweet alyssum, zinnias, and centaureas make fine bedfellows.

whereby flowering annuals were put in and taken out by the hundreds in the gardens of the well-to-do. Jekyll taught that with the knowledge of each perennial's habits and its consequent arrangement in the border according to flowering time and height, a gardener could scatter succeeding volleys of floral color throughout the growing season.

Of special ingenuity in this regard was Jekyll's notion of how to group plants to achieve bold color effects. Departing from previous customs, which called either for planting primarily annual species in regimented and well-defined clumps or for using single plants to introduce spots of color, Jekyll devised the now-familiar method of using drifts of perennials. In a drift, each species is planted in a narrow, curving band set at an oblique angle to the line of the border and subtly interplanted with a few plants from the adjoining drifts on either side. In this way any plant group seen before or after its time has only a minimal presence in the bed, being largely overshadowed by the plants that arise in and around it. When the drift is in flower, however, it unfolds its glories in a continuing sequence of surprises as the viewer walks along the front of the border, seeing it first in full view, then gradually in combination with other flowers and foliage as it recedes and another drift takes its place in the foreground.

Jekyll's border schemes are still studied closely for the wealth of ideas they contain, though few gardeners are willing or able to undertake gardening on the scale she did. Gardeners preferring a more formal look than Jekyll's impressionistic style continue to use colors in more structured ways and to rely more on mixed plantings of annuals and perennials. But there is no question that Jekyll showed the way to redefine the border and explore its wonderful possibilities.

This perennial garden is designed for a succession of bloom. Some sections will be in flower while others are quietly approaching bloom or bowing out. The plants are arranged in graceful drifts that flow easily into one another.

In a semiformal garden on Philadelphia's Main Line three tiers of roses fill a long rectangular bed. In the lowest rank are 'American Independence' miniature roses, in the middle are 'Betty Prior' floribundas and 'Chrysler Imperial' hybrid tea roses, and at the rear are tall white 'Iceberg' floribundas.

This lover's knot border, opposite, is edged with green and variegated forms of Euonymus microphylla.

In this informal border, above, the gardener has opted to let lady's mantle spill over onto the flagstone path.

By the Water

Lucky the gardener whose site is provided with a natural pond, for its still, cool water becomes a ready focal point of garden design, mirroring the sky and the plants along its margins. But natural-looking ponds can also be created artificially in many locations, presuming there is a reliable source of water available and the pond is lined with puddled clay or some other material that will keep the water from seeping out the bottom. Indeed, in some instances, particularly where the existing site is boggy and poorly drained, a well-engineered man-made pond can even be the solution to a gardener's nightmare, becoming a convenient means of drawing off excess water in the surrounding earth. On smaller properties, a simple pool can be created from your own design or with a pre-formed liner.

Certain design principles must be kept in mind, however, in using a pond or pool as an ornamental feature in a garden. A pond should be of sufficient size to look good; any pond less than eight to ten feet in diameter is going to look like a puddle. A simple pool can be smaller. Both ponds and pools should be shaped in a manner that imitates nature, which means no straight lines, but rather something that curves irregularly. The edges should meet the water at a gentle angle so that plants that like their feet in water (blue-flag iris, for example) can be accommodated. And the pond or pool should be scrupulously maintained, which means that leaves must be skimmed off each fall and aquatic plant life kept under control lest it eventually take over the pond altogether. A note of particular caution: Before deciding to add a pond, consult a soil or pond engineer and, in most areas, the appropriate government agencies, such as the local zoning commission and the Department of Environmental Protection, for there are very definite requirements that the

Brilliant blue heliotrope and rose-pink begonias have the edge around this man-made pond. Technically classified as perennials, these tender plants are started indoors and bedded out in spring. They return the kindness with prolific flowering over a long season.

pond builder must meet for such a project.

For gardeners without space for a full-scale pond, a small pool can provide an opportunity to grow waterlilies, lotus, aquatic grasses, and bog plants. Water garden suppliers sell plastic or fiberglass liners in various sizes that are installed in a hole dug in the ground, then filled with water to create the pool. A depth of only 14 to 18 inches is sufficient for many water plants and some fish. The pool liners can also be used to create bog gardens of plants that like to grow in wet soil.

Fountains and waterspills turn water into an element that is pleasing not only to the eye but to the ear and mind, adding sparkle,

A mound of sundrops (Oenothera tetragona), *daytime cousins of the evening primrose, provides a brilliant mass of lemon-yellow color that echoes the yellow flowers at pondside. Vigorous perennials, the sundrops would grow beyond their borders if not kept in check.*

movement, a sense of coolness, a pretty sound, and the feeling of peace that often inspires meditative thought. The scale of water elements can range from the spectacular (the grand *jets d'eau* at Versailles, for example) to the very modest (the trickling water of the bamboo flume in a tiny Japanese garden). It all depends upon the gardener's ambitions, the overall scale of the place, and the water conventions appropriate to the rest of the garden arrangement, i.e., formal fountains in formal gardens, irregular treatments in informal gardens, and the like. Thanks to a variety of ingenious devices, fountains and waterfalls need not even be terribly complicated or expensive to install. One particularly wonderful invention available to the amateur gardener is the submersible recirculating water pump, powered by electricity, that makes it possible to keep a quantity of reserved water flowing over and over again without the need for costly plumbing work and connections to the main water supply of the house.

Perhaps the only significant task you must consider in deciding whether to include a water element in the garden is maintenance. Periodic cleaning of the equipment and replacement of the water are unavoidable chores. In areas of the country subject to seasonal freezing, flowing water systems will also need to be drained and winterized.

In the example shown, part of the formal gardens of Meadowbrook Farm in Meadowbrook, Pennsylvania, the fountain is placed at the center of a formal pool which is itself lined with quarried stone. Another possible way to introduce moving water is to install a wall fountain or spillway in the corner of a garden, the water issuing forth from some height to fall into a small basin or pool below. This is especially practical where existing water lines are already close at hand, as when the garden bed runs along the outside of a house wall that carries interior water lines in close proximity.

Drifts of spiky sage (Salvia) and showy golden yarrow (Achillea filipendulina) provide the main floral display at pond's edge on a late summer day. A scattering of mallows in the foreground softens the effect.

Edible Beds

Vegetables and fruits are often overlooked as sources of decorative flowers and foliage, but the fact is, there are many very showy plants in these categories. By combining them with a few more traditional flowering plants, the gardener can have a bed that provides not only treats for the eye but treats for the palate as well. There is a historical precedent for the mix: The original English cottage gardens, which grew up alongside the modest dwellings of English tenant farmers, were of necessity mixes of the utilitarian and ornamental, with the family's food supply invariably interplanted with gillyflowers, sea pinks, and the like.

There are also some very practical reasons for mixing edibles and flowers. In a situation where full sunlight or space is at a premium, combining edibles and flowers in the same garden may be the only practical way to have both. If a substantial supply of cutting flowers is wanted for decorating the house, and their taking would interfere with the neat appearance of a display flower garden, then creating space for a few cutting flowers in and around the edible garden makes a good deal of sense.

When looking for ornamental edibles, consider the same features you would look for in more conventional annuals and perenni-

Oriental vegetables are given prominence in these beds, opposite. Ornamental cabbage, a hybrid noted for its blush-red heart, takes the foreground.

A "salad" theme animates this lovely backyard garden, above. Eight varieties of lettuce take the center, while low-growing herbs form the edging.

als: leaf texture and color, plant form, flowers, and brightly colored fruits or pods. Among the stand-out vegetables to consider are the ornamental brassicas: cabbages and kales. Nowadays, hybrid cabbages are available in both standard and dwarf sizes, in compact and loose-leafed curly heads, and in colors ranging from the traditional green to cream, pink, red, and blue.

One of four beds of varieties of lettuce, this rectangle features several dozen 'Green Ice' plants. The plants are grown so that a few are ready for harvesting every couple of weeks. The beds are mulched with small chips of red shale, which keep the soil cool and moist while providing color contrast.

Kales and ornamental flowering kale varieties are also good choices. The former have orangey-red flowers, finely curled blue-green leaves, and a compact form that make them ideal edging plants. The latter have flowers as well, but their deeply cut, frilled green foliage turns an extraordinary red at the center as the colder days come on, making them among the more dramatic plants in the fall garden. Rhubarb, a perennial, is typically grown for its sweet, rosy-colored stalks, but its huge green leaves (which are poisonous) and its curious, primitive-looking floral clusters make a grand display from midspring through summer; like any perennial in an edible bed, they are best located off to the side, where they need not be disturbed when the rest of the soil is worked over.

Okra, an edible hibiscus with soft-petaled pale yellow flowers to prove it, includes among its ornamental hybrids one that sports red-veined green leaves and red pods. Eggplants, sweet and hot peppers, and compact patio or "pixie" tomatoes, all with attractive leaves and brilliant fruits in a rainbow of colors, are other good choices for midsized ornamentals. Clumps of lettuce—heading types like Butterhead and Bibb, looseleaf types like Salad Bowl and Ruby, cos types like Romaine, in many fresh tones of green and red—are excellent edging plants. And among the ornamental climbers, suitable for growing on a trellis or fence at the back of a border, are scarlet runner beans, hops, bitter melon, and cucumbers.

Handsome small-fruited perennial plants suitable for the edible border or bed include strawberries and high-bush blueberries. Blueberries grow to 15 feet tall and belong toward the back of a border or at the center of a large, free-standing bed. Another option for a large, sunny bed is a dwarf fruit tree espaliered against a fence or trellis at the back of the bed.

If some fruits and vegetables are often ne-

glected as ornamental plants, so too, some flowers are often forgotten as edibles. Daylilies, for example, produce flower buds that can be eaten raw, as tasty additions to salads, or sautéed lightly as a vegetable; their new shoots make a tender green; their tubers can be prepared like Jerusalem artichokes. And the flowers of nasturtiums and calendulas are also edible in salads or as garnishes.

More than most, the plants in the edible garden need to be easily accessible so they can be weeded, tended, and harvested when ready. Most species require watering fairly often, too.

Roman chamomile, with its feathery foliage and daisylike flowers, provides evergreen edging for a pair of year-round edible borders in this central California garden. Among the notable ornamental vegetables and herbs prospering here are chili peppers, tomatoes, and basil, growing in the raised planter, and a bush variety of zucchini behind them.

Urban Beds and Borders

Urban gardens present a number of unique problems and opportunities for the gardener. On the problem side, city gardens are typically rather small and rectangular, with a terrain that is conventionally flat or nearly so. Carved out of the backyard spaces between row houses and apartment buildings, these pocket gardens also tend to be saddled with a harsh microclimate characterized by little or no air circulation and excessive heat in summer. In the dog days of July and August they can become as hot as an oven; the masonry walls that surround them gather in and hold the kind of heat that wreaks havoc on sensitive plants. Urban gardens are also likely to have highly acidic soil, due to the daily fallout of industrial and auto pollutants. Finally, they often get direct sunlight only at high noon and spend the rest of the day in the shadows of the tall structures that surround them.

But urban gardens can also be quite wonderful in the hands of knowledgeable gardeners, offering oases of peace and greenery where they are most appreciated. And their small size makes even intensive gardening and maintenance relatively easy. Soil conditions are among the first hurdles to overcome. Poor soil can be enriched by carting in a few yards of topsoil, just enough to dress the surface of the beds or to create raised beds. A different strategy is to leave the unsatisfactory soil as is and fill the beds with plants grown in containers that are sunk into the ground, what the English call "the plunging system." In this way, each plant appears to be growing naturally, but it is provided with the kind of soil it likes best with a minimum of earth-moving labor.

Plants should be carefully chosen for the particular challenges the city offers. In general they should be tough, easy to grow, tolerant of atmospheric pollution, relatively heat resistant, and not too demanding in their sun or water requirements. They should also be considered in terms of their aggressiveness; plants that behave like backyard bullies, rapidly spreading where they are not wanted, are to be avoided. And their size and form ought to be evaluated in relation to the space available; large-leaved foliage and flowers work well in the foreground of a small garden, while more diminutive plants placed in the background are surprisingly effective in giving the illusion of greater space overall.

Some of the many highly rated, well-behaved plants that do well in an urban setting are sedums, candytuft, maiden grass, fountain grass, hosta, lamium, coneflowers,

Bricks and fieldstone are combined in a backyard patio garden, above.

A backyard garden in a city setting, opposite, uses its planting space to the maximum.

and lady's mantle. Impatiens, bedded out in spring, is a wonderful source of luminous color. Spring bulbs can also work well. Among the climbing plants to consider are the ivies, climbing hydrangea, and winter-creeper.

The ivies (*Hedera*) are self-clinging perennials that are equipped to grow in almost any soil as ground creepers or climbers, in dark shade or full sun. Climbing hydrangea (*Hydrangea petiolaris*) is a hardy, deciduous, self-attaching climber with large floral clusters. Winter-creeper (*Euonymus fortunei*) is a hardy evergreen climber, producing greenish-white flowers and light pink fruit; one of the more

compact spreading vines, it works especially well in confined locations, and thanks to its small, dark green leaves, it looks good right through the winter. It can also be used as a groundcover.

Vines are, incidentally, of particular value in creating a sense of privacy in the urban garden. Once well established, a vine can be persuaded to cover surrounding property-line walls and fences, turning the rigid geometry of the place into something softer and more inviting. In addition, an arbor or trellis can be added to the garden, either as an extension of the building or as its own freestanding

Astilbe chinensis, *a vigorous perennial, pokes its mauve-pink flower heads above the green surroundings, above.*

A small pool adds grace to this urban space, opposite, providing a hospitable habitat for one of the pygmy forms of water lily.

structure, and the vines coaxed over the framework to make a lush green canopy. Except for those vines that are "self-climbing," vines are likely to need the extra structural support of a lattice frame, built a few inches out from the wall and firmly attached to it. Lattices are also recommended as protection for wooden walls and siding, no matter what the climbing habits of the chosen vine, as wood needs plenty of air circulation to prevent rotting.

Walkways, decking, and patio treatments for the city garden should take into account the size and character of the garden design and the materials of surrounding buildings. In a small space, the usual rule of thumb is to keep the treatment simple and in harmony with what exists; in this way, paths and pav-

ing become the unifying element. Pebbles, wood rounds, and flagstone steppingstones, placed in an irregular and winding design, impart an informal look. Bricks and wooden walkways, laid in a wide variety of patterns, from straight running bond to diagonal, herringbone, and basketweave, are somewhat more formal. Concrete pavers or pebble and stone mosaics, set in a geometrical pattern, tend to be more formal still.

Noise pollution, whether the sound of street traffic or the neighbors' air conditioners, can be effectively obscured by creating another sort of noise—the sound of splashing water. Given the usual scale of the urban garden, the water element can be quite small—a shallow basin made of colored stone or glazed tiles, for example.

Rock Gardens

Rock gardens are the antithesis of flat formal gardens. They celebrate the irregular, the rough, the wild, and the romantic, and they are meant to look as though nature, not man, had the upper hand in creating them. In their purest form, rock gardens are planted with so-called alpines, diminutive mountain-grown plants that are as important for the color and form of their foliage as they are for their flowers. But dwarf evergreens, succulents, woodland wildflowers, ferns, and all sorts of other plants that need good drainage and tolerate thin soil are now included in the wider definition of the term.

Rock gardens are wonderfully versatile and accommodating. Where the existing terrain and soil conditions are already difficult—lots of bedrock outcroppings, a sloping grade, and rather shallow, acidic soil cover-–a rock garden may be the only sensible answer to designing and establishing a garden bed. In such a situation, the gardener will need to do relatively little rearranging of the rocks and soil in situ. But a small, effective rock garden can be created even where the existing terrain is relatively flat if additional rocks and earth are brought in to introduce a small degree of elevation. In the latter instance, the key to suc-

Low-lying alpines planted among granite boulders, above, evoke high-altitude terrain, while making perfect use of a steeply sloped Vancouver yard.

Opuntia basilaris, a species of prickly pear, grows vigorously in this Tucson garden, opposite.

cess lies in observing the examples of undisturbed hillsides in the immediate area and seeing how nature distributes its endowments naturally. Then, perhaps with the help of a garden supply contractor, specimen rocks and boulders can be rounded up from the surrounding countryside. The rocks should be of a single native type, preferably metamorphic rocks like granite and gneiss, and already in their lichen-covered, weathered state; rock that has been recently blasted or fractured is usually unsatisfactory because of its raw, sharp edges.

In setting rocks and boulders in the rock garden, several practical points must be kept in mind. Most of the larger ones belong near the base of the hillock, as gravity would have placed them over time, and most of the smaller ones belong higher up, with only an occasional break in this pattern to make the arrangement look natural. Groupings should appear to be random and irregular in size and number, and each one ought to have its elements sufficiently close to one another so that they will hold planting pockets or terraced beds behind them in the hillside. Positioning each rock is also critical. The general rule of thumb is: Graining or striations of each rock should run in the same general direction as its neighbors, and the base ought to be buried in the earth in such a way that it not only is firm in fact, but looks so. The Japanese, who have done more than any other culture to use rocks and stone effectively in the garden, traditionally bury each specimen to the depth of its spread line, the point of greatest girth. The rock's upper face is tilted ever so slightly so that any rain runoff is directed at the plant

*The showy flowers of elecampane (*Inula Helenium*) grow near the center of this Pacific Northwest rock garden.*

roots behind, and then the prepared soil is packed into the cracks, crevices, and spaces where it can be counted on to stay.

With careful planning, a rock garden can offer a variety of sun, soil, and water conditions, each planting pocket being treated as its own small environment and its plants chosen accordingly.

Plants of true alpine origin need a coarse, gritty soil and moderate sun, such as nature provides on the rocky, windswept slopes of mountains. Some of the outstanding species of alpines are the deep blue harebell (*Campanula alpina*), basket-of-gold (*Aurinia saxatilis*), a number of different low-growth phlox, several species of gentian (*Gentiana*), the pasque-flower (*Pulsatilla patens*), and shooting star (*Dodecatheon meadia*). Woodland wildflowers

and dwarf evergreens generally do better in shadier locations and in heavier soils. Attractive plants for the rock garden include trillium and crocus, as well as creeping juniper, mugo pine (*Pinus mugo*), and dwarf rhododendron. All sorts of succulents, which have specialized structures for storing water, are still another category of plants that adapt well to the rock garden in many regions of the country. The prickly pear (*Opuntia*) has species adapted to just about every part of the United States, which is also true of the sedums, the sempervivums, and the euphorbias.

In choosing rock garden plants, the usual wisdom is to start with those materials that are considered dependable and easy to grow in the area, and distribute them in such a way that there is room for them to reach their growth potential. Bare areas in between can be mulched with natural materials like woodbark to keep down weeds. Then, as experience is gained and the foundation plantings become well established, more temperamental, more elegant accent plants can be put in some of the open spaces. These more unusual plants are usually found through specialty nurseries or through the seed exchanges of plant groups like the American Rock Garden Society. Under no circumstances should amateurs attempt to collect rare plants in the wild, for the majority are now, properly, under the protection of federal and state conservation laws.

A variation on the rock garden theme is a garden planted in association with stone walls. The stone walls are typically laid up against an earthen berm, with the back side of the wall supporting the terraced earth and the front side fully exposed as a garden feature. The favored stone for this purpose is naturally weathered fieldstone, and the traditional way of laying it up is course by course without benefit of mortar, so that small spaces remain between individual stones. Plants can then be grown on the berm behind, with some trailing species trained to grow across the top of the wall and hang down. Still other shallow-rooted plants can actually be tucked into the soil-filled spaces on the vertical face of the wall. The effect is one of natural growth, as though the plants had settled in and on the wall by chance and were gradually reclaiming the space for themselves.

Features of this charming rock garden, opposite, include thyme, covered with pale purple flowers, and stately foxglove with its spikes of rosy pink blooms. Stones were carried up from a nearby ravine and fitted one by one into the hillside before the plantings were begun.

Scores of unusual alpines crowd a rock garden on a stony, shallow-earthed hillside, above. The owners, who concentrate on species of rock garden plants, raise virtually all their specimens from seed in order to assure the purity of their selections.

Herbal Gardens

Herb gardening, which is to say the raising of small, easy-to-cultivate plants of special usefulness, is undoubtedly the oldest form of ornamental gardening practiced in the West. Not only were herbs the earliest source of medicines, culinary flavorings, and fragrances, but they were also clearly associated with magic and religious ceremonies. Beginning in the Middle Ages, such gardens were routinely included within the walls of Christian monasteries, and it was not long before a traditional layout became the garden plan of choice. The large rectangle that was set aside for gardening was divided by grassy or graveled paths into four quarters; where the paths intersected at the center stood a well or some other water feature, handy for watering plants but also well positioned for the enjoyment of the monks and visitors who made the garden their outdoor retreat.

Medicinal and aromatic herbs live in pretty proximity in this formal herb garden, above.

In this informal border of medicinal herbs, opposite, common speedwell shares space with lavender cotton.

The herbs in each quarter might be segregated according to category of use—one containing a collection of medicinal plants, another culinary herbs, another fragrances, and a fourth magical or religious plants. But as time passed these groupings of convenience were often discarded in favor of more elaborate, formal arrangements. These later gardens, which were at their height of popularity during the Renaissance, were characterized by intertwining ribbon rows of herbs laid out to form cartwheels, knots, and other symmetrical patterns. To keep the formal patterns distinctly visible to people wandering along the margins of the gardens, herbs had to be relatively low-growing and amenable to the pruning shears. To dramatize the artistry of the gardener further, spaces between the green ribbons were often filled with flowering perennials and colored gravels.

Modern gardeners may choose to follow the old order, but more personal and contemporary arrangements that combine aesthetics with functional planning can also prove immensely rewarding.

Choosing an effective location is, perhaps, the first decision to make. Close by the kitchen door is good because it puts culinary herbs where they will be convenient for picking on the spur of the moment. But an herb garden is also a wonderful source of fragrance, so a location bordering a much-frequented path, where strollers are likely to brush plants along the edge and release their perfumes, also has a lot to offer as a site.

Two limiting factors in site selection, however, are sun exposure and soil drainage. Most herbs will grow thin and rangy and develop poor flavor without at least five hours of full sun daily, and few can tolerate soggy soil. On the other hand, most herbs are rather drought resistant and thrive in soil of only

average fertility. They do need to be weeded from time to time, and some perennial herbs must be cut back each fall to keep them from taking over their less aggressive neighbors, but the doing here tends to be a pure delight to the senses.

Choosing among the literally hundreds of annual and perennial herbs available can be difficult for the novice. A logical way to begin is to settle on a single theme, and for most people, the theme of greatest continuing interest is kitchen herbs. A basic list of culinary herbs might include basil, bay, chervil, chives, coriander or cilantro, dill, marjoram, mint, oregano, parsley, rosemary, sage, savory, tarragon, and thyme. Other tried and proven themes include fragrance beds, beds for dried winter arrangements, beds created in line with specific historical traditions, and silver or grey gardens. This last theme garden, which can be extraordinarily beautiful on a moonlit night as well as in daytime, might begin with silvery yarrow, a number of artemisias, lavender, lavender cotton, lamb's ear, woolly mint, globe thistle, and silver sage. Seed catalogues and plant nurseries offer a broad selection of the most popular herbs; for more unusual species and cultivars, herb societies as well as historical house and garden museums are excellent sources of both seeds and seedlings.

Bold drifts of white daisylike flowers of the herb feverfew (Chrysanthemum parthenium) *dominate the rear of this informal bed. The plant was long regarded as a remedy for all sorts of fevers and as an air purifier, especially good for planting around the doors and windows of houses. Here it blends its pleasant fragrance with thyme, speedwell, and lavender cotton.*

The Wild Look

The ultimate in informal gardening is, by some accounts, "the wild look," a style that seems to have been created entirely by and for Mother Nature. But the wildness is all appearances. Actually, to achieve the most effective naturalistic look the gardener must exercise exquisite taste and restraint in assembling and arranging materials.

The basic elements of a wild garden are seemingly random plantings of annuals, perennials, and bulbs, a few well-chosen specimens of native trees and shrubbery, and here and there swatches of easy-care ground covers. Bed shapes must be informal, too, with rough edging—often ledge or fieldstone—along irregular front edges.

While the wild garden is sometimes the dominant theme of the landscape, many gar-

Trees and tall shrubs provide the rich green background for this somewhat wild-looking backyard garden in Atlanta, above.

This border, opposite, is alive with an assortment of flowering and foliage plants, arranged in informal rows that rise with the changing terrain.

deners with larger areas to work with find delight in creating dual zones, in which more formal beds are located near the house and patio and more naturalistic gardens are placed some distance away, at the far side of a broad lawn or pond and, preferably, in a location that marks some natural transition in the terrain, like a hillside or the edge of a woods. Thus, the wild bed provides a point of interest in the distance, drawing the eye to the farther reaches of the usable landscape to say, in effect, "here is where nature takes over from the hand of man."

As to particular plant selections, the general rule of thumb is to have the majority of plants native to the area. Not only do natives have a high probability of taking hold vigorously, but they just look as though they belong there. And simple, unsophisticated flowers, only once remove from their wild ancestors, are generally considered more effective than complex forms, with double flowers and bright, modern colors.

From early spring until late fall, the courtyard of this Norman-style house is enveloped in color and fragrance. Notable among the exuberant tall perennials that frame the entrance are clematis and a species of climbing rose.

On a city lot in Vancouver, beneath the shade of 100-ft. cedars, a wonderful assortment of green- and silver-leafed woodland plants, left, thrives year round. Notable in this picture are the blood-red cranesbill and spotted dead nettle, as well as two varieties of hosta, and English primrose.

Complementing the more formal gardens that skirt the house proper, this wild garden on a lower terrace, opposite, is filled with vigorous, self-seeding hardy perennials that jostle one another for space. Among the pretty contenders are coral bells, Carolina lupine, daylilies, and foxglove.

Reminiscent of a flowering meadow, this pastoral border, above, combines a quartet of traditional country bloomers including blanket flowers, bellflowers, foxglove, and cottage pinks.

Green Gardens

Variegated hostas and strawberry geraniums provide an abundance of green against the dark red backdrop of a basket-weave brick wall, above.

Cool, lush, and very inviting, the island bed, opposite, combines the arching bluish green blades of Mondo grass (Ophiopogon japonicus) with the yellow-green of Gumpo azaleas growing in profusion at center.

Ornamental garden beds usually evoke thoughts of flowering annuals and perennials, but a green garden made up of bold and theatrical-looking green and silver-green foliage plants can be a delightful and unusual alternative. And because foliage plants enjoy a longer season, some looking well throughout all twelve months of the year, they are worth considering where year-round appearance is important.

Green gardens are typically planted out with a number of different foliage species, their selections based upon contrasting and complementary plant forms and leaf shapes, textures, markings, and shades of green to silver (plants which flower somewhat inconspicuously or very briefly may also be included). Probably because we associate the color green with nature, a green garden can be counted on to create an atmosphere of tranquility and restfulness. In the South and Southwest, where green gardens are particularly popular, they are also appreciated for their ability to cool their surroundings visually, a psychological phenomenon based on the fact that green is a cool color, located on the side of the spectrum opposite from hot colors.

A foliage garden can offer surprising variety. There are many shades of green whose subtle differences can be appreciated when placed in close proximity to one another. There are deep forest greens, soft blue-greens, and light springlike chartreuse shades to add interest to the garden. And there are many kinds of variegated leaves—striped, splashed, spotted, and edged in creamy white, yellow, gold, even red or pink—that extend the palette as well.

In addition to the delicate shadings of color, a green garden is a perfect place to notice the textures and shapes of leaves. The big, bold leaves of hostas, for example, are vastly different from the feathery foliage of a maidenhair fern, the dramatically spiky leaves of a yucca, or the soft, downy leaves of lamb's ears. In a flower garden the flowers are the stars, but in a green garden the leaf forms and textures which are so often overlooked add richness and depth to the design. Foliage gardens can be serene places of quiet beauty.

At the top of the list of favorite foliage plants used in green gardens are hostas, which in their incredible diversity of leaf size and variegated leaf patterns are unmatched as ground covers. Some other "greens" are alchemilla, bergenia, boxwood, camellia, cotoneaster, fatsia, gunnera, hellebore, holly, ornamental rhubarb, osmanthus, and flax. Among the silver- and grey-tinted foliage plants are artemisia, cardoon, daisy bush, lamb's ears, lavender, santolina, senecio, and yucca. Ferns, including maidenhair ferns, are another category of plants to investigate.

A green garden can be described as a kind of theme garden in which the gardener's choices are focused not so much on the selection of individual plants as on the creation of an overall effect, in this case a display of cooling greens. The theme may be carried throughout the property if the gardener chooses, but many prefer to create other themes in other parts of the garden if there is space enough to keep the separate elements from competing. Among myriad theme possibilities are other monochromatic color schemes—all white flowers, all blue, etc.— as well as a fragrance garden, a winter garden, a rose garden, a butterfly garden, and a Victorian garden, each treated according to its own set of requirements.

Ilex has been planted as a circle within a circle in this Savannah garden. Thanks to careful shearing, the inner circle has been shaped to indicate the cardinal points of the compass.

The smooth, shiny, heart-shaped leaves of hostas, also known as plantain lilies, contrast attractively here with the red-veined, matte leaves of saxifrage, opposite. Each plant flowers only briefly, but the foliage pairings will remain interesting throughout the growing season.

Six varieties of hosta, in several variegation patterns and assorted shades of green, are bedded around twin tree trunks, above, to form a handsome composition of subtle colors and textures.

Centerpieces

A combination birdbath and sundial stands at the center of a colonial-style garden in Oregon, above. Its fluted base is surrounded by concentric bands of the dwarf Japanese barberry 'Crimson Pygmy' and a compact variety of green santolina.

Centering on a traditional armillary sphere, this beautifully scaled formal garden, opposite, uses mellow terra-cotta brick to describe a circle within a square courtyard. Beds are planted with relatively small-scale materials such as geraniums and Gumpo azaleas, with low-growing ivy as a tidy edging.

Ornamental features as the focal point of garden design are an ancient tradition, going back at least to medieval times and probably before. They continue to play a role in many contemporary formal gardens, lending order and elegance to the garden composition.

In the beginning, the primary purpose of such features was largely utilitarian—a fountain or spigot to mark the outlet of an underground spring that serviced the garden, a heraldic figure or mythical god to protect the place. These were followed by a host of other devices whose value was to delight the eye and the imagination. The sundial, fixed upon a pedestal or a garden wall, was one of the standard ornaments in English and Scottish gardens beginning in the sixteenth century; it continued to be used centuries after the clock and pocket watch had long ago made it obsolete.

Marble and stone statues first found favor on the Continent during the Renaissance; they crossed the Channel in the seventeenth century, often becoming rather whimsical fixtures—nymphs, cherubs, shepherds—in the gardens of the English upper classes. Vases and urns were borrowed from the classical age; oversized versions of ancient funerary urns, they came to symbolize eternity, a concept in keeping with the notion of the garden as a place to contemplate life's mysteries.

In the nineteenth century, mass-produced lead, cast iron, and terra-cotta versions of all these ornaments came along to satisfy the growing popular market. Last, and in a sense representing a return to the utilitarian, the birdbath was introduced as a stylish garden ornament at the beginning of the twentieth century.

Care should be taken in using any of these elements, even if one is fortunate enough to find an antique or a good reproduction. Prob-

ably the greatest pitfall is in determining the proper scale of the ornament, which must be sufficient to become a focus of attention in a particular space. There really are no fixed rules on this, but continued observation of successful (and unsuccessful) installations will gradually build a sense of what is needed; be aware, however, that most mistakes are made on the side of under scale.

The most usual placement for a garden ornament is at a central location—where paths come together or at the center of the lawn between two balanced beds. Other placements to consider are an accent to a pool or pond, in matched pairs on either side of an entryway, in a niche within a wall or a formal hedge, or at the end of a path as a way to draw the eye to a distant vista.

Blue and white pansies complement the colors of an Italian glazed terra-cotta pot, above, giving each element an extra measure of brilliance. The bed is the centerpiece of a patio whose surface material—reused sections of an old greenhouse floor—have been set radially to create a strong pattern around the pot.

The merry sounds of trickling water animate this garden centerpiece, opposite. The fountain, a reproduction of an old English piece, is made in the form of a tiny bird. The receptacle below is made of terra-cotta to match the brick background.

Old-Fashioned Beds

An old-fashioned bed, as most of us under-stand the term, is not so much a matter of style as it is of plant choice. It depends for its romantic, soft beauty on what the English used to call cottage flowers, so named for their long association with rural English dwellings, where for centuries they were grown, somewhat hit-and-miss, in the front yards of country cottages, along with the family's herbs, vegetables, and fruits.

These mixed floral borders have been under the tender care of their owner-gardener for nearly half a century, during which time a great diversity of perennials, bulbs, shrubs, and trees has prospered.

Two Victorian favorites—foxglove and Siberian iris—raise their dainty heads above a mixed collection of old-fashioned perennials and biennials, opposite.

Cottage flowers are typically steadfast, hardy perennials and biennials, characterized by simple arrangements of flowers in pastel or pure colors, and growth habits that are informal and spontaneous in appearance. Most of these species are native to England, or were introduced so many centuries ago as to seem indigenous there, and grow best in temperate-zone gardens. Most are well known today, though perhaps not always in their old-fashioned, pre-hybrid forms.

Some of the sentimental favorites for the old-fashioned bed or border are hollyhocks, columbines, artemisias, Michaelmas daisies, delphiniums, campanulas, border carna-

tions, foxgloves, iris, purple loosestrife, Oriental poppies, veronica, daylilies, lupines, primroses, tulips, sage, and peonies.

In keeping with the democratic spirit of the old-fashioned garden, traditional shrubs such as lilacs, forsythias, and shrub roses also deserve mention. Climbing and rambling roses add a decidedly romantic touch as they clamber over arbors, trellises, or wooden fences, and their sweet fragrance mingles with those of other scented flowers. For the gardener who likes a different sort of challenge, a pair of espaliered fruit trees, supported along the back wall, makes the nicest sort of vertical accent, and very "cottage" at that.

Two views of this old-fashioned bed, above and opposite, put it in perspective. One of a pair of 10-ft. × 40-ft. beds, it serves to define and enclose an outdoor living space, which is bounded by the house, woodlands, and a swimming pool. Harking back to days of garden parties, the backyard is designed for relaxed summer activities. The plantings include many traditional favorites in a polychrome palette that is predominantly white, blue, lavender, and yellow.

Woodland Gardens

A green-and-white-striped ornamental grass, Arrhenatherum bulbosum, *helps provide a gentle transition from the lawn to the taller, more structured growth in the woodland bed.*

Against a foundation planting of broad-leafed evergreens and mature cedars, the various shrubs and flowers in the foreground, opposite, provide a bright contrast.

Long before meadows were giving way to cultivated lawns, the surrounding woodlands were nature's beds and borders. Cool, damp, alternately sun-dappled and shady, the woodland edges were a gentle sort of frontier between the field-growing wildflowers and the shade-loving undergrowth of the deep, dark, mysterious forest. In a sense, these fringe areas offered the best of both worlds, and over the centuries they have been admired and imitated repeatedly by man.

The owner of a property gifted with mature woodland has an ideal situation for creating a woodland garden. Indeed, to do anything different would be to ignore a valuable asset. But seeing the property for what it can become may be difficult at the outset, so the first step in designing the garden is to undertake some judicious clearing of brambles and underbrush, and then, progressively, to remove a few of the less-favored tree specimens. Gradually, the informal groupings of the remaining trees and native shrubbery will begin to assert themselves and the outlines of the garden-to-be emerge.

Once the basic shape and extent of the bed is worked out, the next step is to determine whether a path might be appropriate and where it might go. Very small beds, sheltered under the canopy of a single clutch of paper birches, for example, are best seen entirely from the periphery and need no path. A larger woodland garden that encircles numbers of trees and varied terrain will benefit from having a meandering path and possibly a bench.

Soil conditions should also be examined closely, as the plant materials that are typically used in woodland gardens—true wildflowers or first-generation species—are often very choosy about the kinds of conditions they require. In general, woodland sites are acidic, the result of generations of leaves de-

composing. But pockets within the site may be notably moister, drier, more acidic or alkaline, and these should be noted.

In selecting and placing plant materials it is useful to think in terms of the way nature does things—drifts of some plants, pockets of others—and to consider the composition in several vertical zones. The lowest zone begins literally at ground level with mosses and lichens and wild woodland flowers such as common varieties of windflower, snakeroot, lady's slipper, foxglove, trailing arbutus, trillium, phlox, lily of the valley, and iris. It rises a few feet to the shrub zone with azaleas, rhododendrons, mountain laurel, and witch hazel, then to the height of slender seedling trees, with their delicate, fresh green leaves and stems, then to the understory that includes such flowering woodland trees as wild dogwood, and finally to the overstory zone, where the canopy of mature deciduous trees becomes another feature in the design.

Under the shade of overhanging trees, delicate flowers and small shrubs, opposite, compete for glory throughout the growing season. Among the standouts shown here are the shrub Cotinus coggyria *'Royal Purple' (smoke tree), the perennial alchemilla, and hardy geraniums.*

Red rhododendron, basket-of-gold, and blue Jacob's ladder provide splashes of brilliant color against the rich greens of this wooded clearing, above.

Raised Beds and Borders

The raised bed is a freestanding garden bed that has been constructed several inches above the natural terrain. The usual reason for raising the site is to provide a better environment for growing, either to lift roots above heavy, poorly draining soil or to introduce a wholly different sort of soil, with an amended pH, to accommodate plants that would not naturally thrive there. But there are several other equally valid reasons for going to the extra effort of bringing in earth and building containing walls or edges.

Raised beds can be used as dividers between one section of the garden and another, creating a more visible barrier than a ground-level bed of comparable size. Raised beds are also somewhat better protected against the casual trespasser or wayward dog, a point to keep in mind where beds are close to heavy traffic areas. Raised beds are less subject to invasion by tree roots and aggressive lawn grasses. Their soil warms up weeks before surrounding soil. And once constructed, raised beds are more convenient to tend and enjoy, being several inches closer to hands and eyes.

The traditional raised bed is an above-ground planting border or bed, at least 8 to 10 inches high, contained on four sides by railroad ties, landscape timbers, a dry stone wall, or some other formal or informal construction. A variation on the raised border is the retaining wall, contained on three sides, and built into an existing slope on the fourth; this construction works well as a transitional element in a space that would otherwise seem to have no coherence: At the upper level the border appears to be at ground level, while on the lower level it is seen as a raised construction.

Rubblestone atop rubblestone makes a low-tech frame for a raised border. Laid without mortar, stones are canted inward for stability.

A raised bed for a New England farmhouse is laid up according to traditional dry-wall construction techniques, using flat fieldstones in staggered courses. The added height accentuates the bed's transitional role between lawn and tall hedges in the back.

An allied, more naturalistic approach to the raised border or bed is to skip containing walls altogether and create an artificial hillock. Simply select your site, outline the shape desired, and drop a load of good soil on the target, raking it out until you have a gently rounded, rock-free mound. For best effect it should stand about 24 to 36 inches near the center and slope gradually to meet the surrounding terrain, at which point a sub-merged weed barrier is advisable.

The size of the bed is largely a matter of choice, though considerations of scale—the proportion of the bed in relationship to the space around it—should not be overlooked in planning. The minimal height of the bed should be sufficient to allow plants to set roots as far down as needed without reaching the unsatisfactory soil base beneath. At least 12 inches is usually recommended, though 18

Large boulders retain a raised bed on a hillside overlooking Oregon's Willamette Valley, above. In this area, where winters are very wet and local clay soil tends to become waterlogged, the raised bed improves drainage and saves the plants from root rot.

The grey stone wall of this raised bed beautifully complements the pink, rose, and purple flowers growing in the front of the bed, opposite.

This garden is located atop a very thin layer of original soil. To provide a good medium for plants, the gardener built raised beds and enhanced the soil in them with "mushroom soil," a very light, rich, natural additive found locally.

inches may be necessary where the ground beneath is exceedingly wet and heavy. Bulbs, in particular, need the extra depth in wet situations.

A soil mixture suitable to the requirements of the intended plants is then prepared, any errant stones or weeds discarded, and the results used to fill the raised bed retaining frame. Plants may then be set in place in the usual fashion. Given the superior quality of the soil, most raised bed gardeners find that their gardens do best when they plant intensively, with a minimum of space between neighbors.

Dry stone walls, in which stones are carefully fitted together without mortar, are difficult to build but make lovely edgings for a raised bed.

Propagation beds, above, made of 2-in. × 10-in. lumber set in trenches for extra firmness, are as decorative as they are useful. Here they support communities of rare alpines, raised from seed in preparation for planting out in permanent beds.

Grey paving bricks, a Savannah tradition, enclose this raised bed, opposite, which is planted chiefly with shade- and moisture-loving species, including showy, large-leafed acanthus and white astilbe. Neatly clipped boxwood forms the edging.

Terraced Beds

On sloping or irregular terrain, grading is one way to tame a garden site. But a more interesting alternative is to divide the area into two or more terraced levels. By the same token, terrain that starts out absolutely flat and without surprises can be made more inviting by the deliberate introduction of changes of level. Each terraced level then becomes its own space, with the potential to be used and enjoyed in different ways. And because only part of the garden can be fully seen at any level, terracing is also a very useful device for creating the illusion of greater space.

Terracing does not come cheaply. At the very least it involves the construction of retaining walls set into the hillside, and because such walls must support a great deal of unstable weight and accommodate both surface and underground drainage from the slope, they must be carefully engineered and constructed. In some communities owners must secure a building permit before undertaking a retaining wall, and undergo inspections to insure that the work is done according to safety standards. The materials used range from pressure-treated landscape ties, which are guaranteed against rotting for forty years, to dry stone walls and brick masonry.

Another important feature of terracing, or of all slopes for that matter, are steps or stairs to join the different levels. In the hands of an accomplished garden designer steps and stairs are strong design elements, conducting movement visually and in actual fact. As a rule, steps and stairs should be built on a more generous scale than that employed indoors, with broad treads and low risers that lend themselves to a slow thoughtful pace, or even to sitting. But the design must also be in keeping with the mood of the beds themselves, which means straight, evenly spaced stairs, accented perhaps by flanking urns, in association with formal arrangements, and a freer plan for informal gardens.

A rise of only a few inches becomes the opportunity for notching a narrow brick-faced bed into the space between upper and lower lawns. Its owner has filled it with a merry assortment of California poppies, Persian buttercups, nemesia and valerian.

An inviting approach to this house, opposite, combines terraced beds on either side of natural stone steps that climb the rise at an angle. Pretty little plants such as rockrose, basket-of-gold, and spurge are encouraged to grow in the crevices of the steps, making a soft, aromatic but resilient cushion underfoot.

Clouds of white perennial candytuft spill over the wall edging this springtime garden. Pink and red rhododendrons are in full, magnificent bloom in the background.

Multilevel flower beds climb the embankment on either side of a brick entryway. By scaling the height of each terrace to roughly three stairs, the designer has assured a pleasing consistency.

Formal Beds and Borders

Adjoining a restored early–nineteenth-century Georgia plantation house is this recreation of an old-time "flower yard." As befits its period, the patterned garden uses English boxwood as a natural edging for beds that feature pansies and anemones in spring, plumbago and torenia in summer. Stands of American holly, decorative in all seasons, provide vertical accents along the picket fence.

The modern formal garden border is a distant descendant of the gardens of Renaissance Italy and of their somewhat later French refinements. As in times past, the emphasis is usually on the architecture of the place, with each garden being treated as an outdoor room. Beds are almost always geometric in shape, often laid out in matched pairs, and defined by walls or clipped hedges. Instead of being placed on the basis of the property's best site or best exposure, they are typically positioned in precise and balanced relationship to the house, a grand window, or an important entryway, and they are often most effective when seen from some elevation where their patterned plantings become more apparent.

Paths, which are important but low-keyed features of the formal garden, follow crisp, neat lines, and act as links between separate garden areas. Trellises, arches, and arbors, overgrown with climbing vines or actually formed out of sheared and pruned shrubs or trees, are used as devices to frame a fine view or as focal points on their own account. So, too, urns, sundials, sculptures, and water features may be introduced as accents. Illusions of size and distance, what the French call *trompe l'oeil*, are still another traditional feature of the formal garden, and used with skill they are both effective and fun. In their simplest form, the illusions are achieved by forced perspective lines—borders, paths, lattices, archways, and the like are actually made narrower as they recede from a principal viewing place—and the deft use of scale: slightly oversized foliage and ornaments in the foreground, slightly underscale foliage and ornaments in the distance. But subtlety must be the byword, for if the illusions are overdone they quickly become foolish rather than formal.

Plant possibilities are almost unlimited, though most formal gardeners prefer species that have a compact, firm growing habit, or that submit unobtrusively to pruning. In the older, more traditional formal gardens, low-growing evergreens like boxwood, germander, rosemary, and lavender are used to frame the forward edges of a border or bed. Formal gardens are also hospitable to annuals, which may be planted as seeds but are more often bedded out (i.e., grown in a greenhouse and planted out in spring or summer) when the danger of frost has passed and the plants are near to flowering.

Some of the most sturdy but showy bedding annuals are ageratums, celosias, China-

Matched semicircular beds surround and frame an old-fashioned Exeter sundial in this north-facing Charleston townhouse garden. The predominant greens of the garden are shade-loving English ivy (Hedera helix), in a range of leaf forms and sizes. The color accents are white pansies and ruby begonias.

asters, dwarf dahlias, gazanias, geraniums, heliotropes, impatiens, lantanas, lobelias, marigolds, verbenas, and zinnias. As with the perennials, the annuals are planted in discrete, orderly patterns in sufficient numbers of any one species to make a strong, coherent statement. Probably the only category of plant that does not seem appropriate is wildflowers, which, by definition, are not congenial with the highly civilized spirit of the formal garden.

Scrupulous maintenance of the formal border or bed is essential to its success. Most especially, weeds, spent blossoms, and decayed leaves must be removed on a regular basis. And if bedding plants are part of the scheme, they should be retired and replaced when past their prime.

An ornamental belvedere serves as the focal point of this "allée" or promenade, above. The beds that line the allée narrow as they drop from one level to the next, part of an intentional effort to exaggerate perspective and make the outdoor room seem larger than it is. Statuary, ivy topiary, and pompom-pruned junipers are other traditional features here.

Part of the formal grounds of a historic Charleston house, this horseshoe-shaped bed, opposite, occupies the lower of two garden sites. The beds are a carefully orchestrated mix of annuals, perennials, dwarf trees, and shrubs, planned for year-round bloom.

The Dry Garden

Prickly pears (Opuntia) are the dominant plant specimens in the contemporary Phoenix garden, above. The cactuses thrust their large flat pads every which way, catching the sun on their many surfaces to create a handsome play of light and shadow.

This Tucson garden, opposite, closely follows the tenets of Xeriscaping, with plenty of mulching, a minimalist water-delivery system buried underground, and a wide-ranging assortment of desert plants, including moss verbena and desert marigold. The stockade fence in the background is made of lengths of ocotillo. Though the cut canes are not precisely planted in the ground, many of them will root after a few months, forming an extraordinary living wall.

A dry garden describes any gardening scheme that concentrates on drought-resistant plants. Once considered a somewhat eccentric sort of choice even in desert and semidesert locales, when water was used as though it were in limitless supply, the dry garden has become the mode of choice in the southwestern part of the United States and is rapidly gaining adherents in many other sections as well.

Proponents of this kind of conservation gardening have given it the formal name of Xeriscaping, after the Greek word *xeros*, meaning dry. They are so serious about spreading its environmental message that they have established a national advisory council to encourage garden education programs, and they have formulated what they regard as the seven fundamental rules by which gardeners can judge their success in achieving Xeriscape goals. These are: proper planning and design, limited turf or—better yet—terracing in association with beds, efficient irrigation such as submerged drip lines, soil improvements to improve the retention of below-ground moisture, the use of mulches to diminish surface loss of moisture, appropriate maintenance, and finally, the use of plants that need less moisture.

The largest category of Xeriscape plants is succulents, including cactuses, which are the most prevalent forms of native vegetation that grow in the full sun, dry soils, and hot temperatures of the southwestern United States. Succulents are plants that hold water in their fleshy leaves as a means of surviving long dry spells. Cactuses constitute a huge subcategory of succulents, distinguished by their lack of conventional leaves and their exaggerated stems, where water is stored. A cactus garden may not sound terribly enticing to you, but the plants come in a broad array of shapes and sizes. For example, there are

the flat oval pads of opuntias, the round squat shapes of mammillarias, and the spiny barrel cactuses. Many cactuses are covered with bristles and spines, sometimes in decorative white or gold. And many cactuses flower each year, bejeweling themselves with diaphanous or satiny blossoms in rich shades of yellow, pink, red, white, and other colors.

Many other sorts of plants have also been shown to be excellent dry garden ornamentals in recent years. Some outstanding candidates among shrubs are jojoba, firecracker plant, red yucca, purple hop bush, sagebrush, and *Salvia Greggii*, a species of bush sage. Some of the newer choices among perennials are yellow-flowering brittlebush and

Along California's central coast, several species of sword-leafed agaves, and a single primordial-looking crassula bursting into brilliant cordal blossom, provide the horticultural drama. Lower-growing plants include sempervivums, sedums, and portulaca.

desert marigold. California poppies and pen-stemons have also been found suitable for dry gardens. A great deal of work is contin-uing at horticultural laboratories to breed high-performance Xeriscape plants of many other sorts, as well. Gardeners interested in com-prehensive collections of Xeriscape plants will find specialist nurseries and some university horticultural facilities their best bet.

A medley of textures—the wiry stalks of ocotillo, the juicy, prickled pads of opuntias, the feathery leaves of mesquite, and the tender, papery little flowers of bougainvillea—plays nicely on this desert terrace.

CHAPTER

3 Hortus Prospectus

*T*he following list consists of some sixty herbaceous flowering perennials and bulbs, which is to say plants that can be expected to return their flowery favors year after year in most parts of the United States and Canada. For the gardener just getting started, the selections are names to be trusted; most of them are relatively easy to grow in most climates and have an outstanding character as either a flowering or foliage plant or both. But please don't stop here. Think of the list as just a framework to which you will want to add many of your own discoveries, for there are literally thousands of other perennials and bulbs out there to try, not to mention countless rewarding annuals, herbs, ornamental vegetables, shrubs, cactuses, and more.

To broaden your horizons and deepen your experience, take your lead from what successful gardeners in your area are growing. Go on garden tours and, when you see something you like, make notes, and don't be afraid to experiment boldly on your own from time to time. Plant catalogues from reputable nurseries are an invaluable source of new gardening ideas and plant cultivars.

The plant listings here are based upon the standard botanical system of scientific nomenclature. The first word identifies the genus, or group, to which the plant belongs and with which it shares many broad genetic characteristics. The second name, if any, identifies its species, which more narrowly defines the particular plant on the basis of some outstanding characteristic, such as its bushiness, its peculiar ability to attract bees, or its woolly leaves. Now and then, the plant will also be further defined by a third word in single quotation marks, which designates the species as a cultivar or hybrid. Cultivars and hybrids are plants that have been "improved" by human intervention, through either crossbreeding or selection, to produce a color, form, or hardiness not previously found in the natural species. The common name is given in parentheses.

The information included here regarding plant habits, colors, sizes, flowering times, and hardiness zones should be taken as generalizations rather than absolute certainties. Your soil conditions, your local microclimate, the nursery or seed company from which plants originate, and the hands-on care you give your garden will all influence the way your garden grows.

USDA Plant Hardiness Zone Map

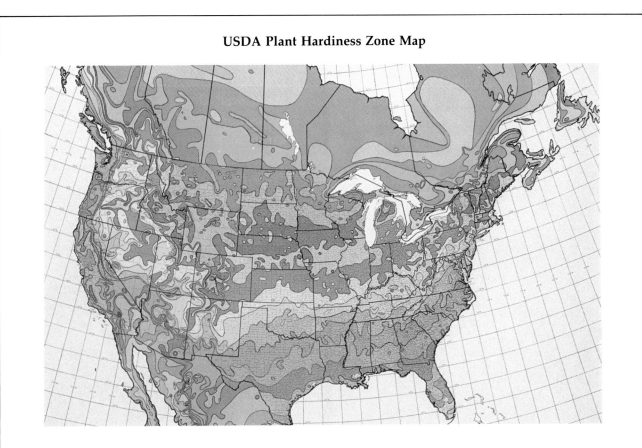

AVERAGE ANNUAL MINIMUM TEMPERATURE

Temperature (°C)	Zone	Temperature (°F)
−45.6 and Below	1	Below −50
−42.8 to −45.5	2a	−45 to −50
−40.0 to −42.7	2b	−40 to −45
−37.3 to −40.0	3a	−35 to −40
−34.5 to −37.2	3b	−30 to −35
−31.7 to −34.4	4a	−25 to −30
−28.9 to −31.6	4b	−20 to −25
−26.2 to −28.8	5a	−15 to −20
−23.4 to −26.1	5b	−10 to −15
−20.6 to −23.3	6a	−5 to −10
−17.8 to −20.5	6b	0 to −5
−15.0 to −17.7	7a	5 to 0
−12.3 to −15.0	7b	10 to 5
−9.5 to −12.2	8a	15 to 10
−6.7 to −9.4	8b	20 to 15
−3.9 to −6.6	9a	25 to 20
−1.2 to −3.8	9b	30 to 25
1.6 to −1.1	10a	35 to 30
4.4 to 1.7	10b	40 to 35
4.5 and above	11	40 and above

Achillea (yarrow). This member of the daisy family has silver-grey, fernlike foliage and attractive flowers that are typically presented in flat, upturned clusters. Developed from the wild white yarrow, most of the garden hybrids are tints and shades of yellow, with a few of the newer colors tending toward more vivid reds and pinks. Individual plants are somewhat open and erect, but in groups they present a bushy appearance due to their dense foliage. Yarrow flowers from late June to August, with good repeat blooms until hard frost if dead-headed regularly. These flowers are excellent for cutting and may be dried for winter bouquets. They prefer full sun and moist, well-drained soil, but will tolerate somewhat less favorable conditions quite well. Yarrow has a tendency to spread vigorously over time, and may need dividing periodically in spring. Except for *A. tomentosa* (woolly yarrow), a low variety suitable for rock gardens and fronts of borders, most yarrows are 2' to 3' tall, suitable in middle-to-rear locations. They are hardy in zones 3–8.

Aconitum (monkshood). Helmet-like flowers are borne on tall spikes with underpinnings of dark, glossy foliage. Flowers are most often lavender to bright blue, though some white and yellow varieties are also available. Monkshoods make fine back-row plants, in that they tend to be exceptionally tall; Wilson's azure monkshood, for example, can reach 6'–8'. For midrange monkshoods, 'Bressingham Spire' is an unusual 3' exception. Monkshoods prefer rich, deep, moist soil in which they set uncommonly deep (and poisonous) roots, partial shade, and staking in exposed locations. They are hardy in zones 3–8.

Alchemilla (lady's mantle). Encompassing more than 200 species, alchemillas are members of the rose family. Their popular name, bestowed in medieval times, reflects the almost pleated, hence mantle-like, appearance of their leaves, which are greyish green, velvety, and as much as 6" in diameter. Delicate, fluffy, greenish-yellow star-shaped flowers, which stand well above leaves on 12"–18" stems, begin appearing in early summer and last through August. Lady's mantles spread readily, becoming almost weedy if not tended. They grow in most soils of average fertility in sun or partial shade, though they prefer shade in hotter, drier climates. Use them at the front edge of a border as the lowest tier of plantings or as an excellent ground cover in zones 3–9.

Allium (ornamental onion). This genus includes a great variety of unusual flower shapes. *A. Christophii* is notable for its oversized globular head of pale violet stars that stands 18" high, atop floppy onion leaves. *A. senescens*, a smaller form, puts up pink flowers on 8" stems. Alliums like full sun in zones 3–9.

Anemone blanda (windflower). A tuberous-rooted member of the large buttercup family, *A. blanda* produces daisy-shaped flowers that appear in May soon after crocuses and scilla. Some varieties are an intense blue, others white, scarlet, or cyclamen pink. They grow 3"–8" tall, depending upon the strain, which makes them nicely proportioned for a rock garden. They want partial to full sun in zones 5–8.

Anemone × hybrida (Japanese anemone). This anemone species is a late-bloomer, with 2"–3" pink or white single or double flowers appearing from late summer to midfall. Their leaves are also handsome; dark to light green and shaped somewhat like a maple leaf with deep lobes, they cover the plant densely at the base and become smaller and fewer toward the top. A long slender stem, as much as 1' to 2' long, carries the many-branched

Anemone pulsatilla (*pasqueflower*)

flower stalks. *A. vitifolia*, the grape-leaved anemone, shares many points in common with the Japanese anemone, but bears single, deep pink flowers only. They like light shade and moist, well-drained soil. They also need a location that is protected from prevailing winds and need winter protection in more northerly areas. They are hardy in zones 5–8.

Anemone pulsatilla (*pasqueflower*). A spring flower whose membership in the anemone family is somewhat in dispute, these "probable" anemones are early blooming dwarfs that prefer part shade and rich, woodland soil. They rarely exceed 12″ in height and produce lavender to purple flowers on fringed leaves. Some nurseries have also developed white and red cultivars in recent years. Hardy to zone 4 or 5.

Anthemis tinctoria (*golden marguerite*). One of the longer-flowering perennials, golden marguerites bear sizable, yellow daisylike blossoms all summer and into early fall with no more care than dead-heading. The 2′–3′ tall plants are characterized by a bushy form and handsome, fernlike foliage. They need full

sun and well-drained soil, and are hardy to zone 3.

Aquilegia (*columbine*). Columbines are pastel-colored spring garden staples. They bear distinctive five-petaled flowers atop a set of sepals that may be of matching or contrasting colors. The back of each petal has a pronounced spur, a peculiar appendage that is sometimes likened to an eagle's claw (*aquilegia* comes from the Latin word for eagle); filled with nectar in season, the spurs draw hummingbirds. Most columbines grow between 18″ and 36″ tall, though some hybrids are as low as 6″. Their foliage consists of notched dark green or blue-green compound leaves that have a fine-textured appearance from a distance. Due to their early flowering season, they should be combined with plants whose oncoming foliage will camouflage their fading remains come July in an all-summer border or bed. Native to the woodlands, hybrid columbines still favor moist, well-drained soil in very light shade, but will tolerate full sun where there is adequate moisture. Perennial in zones 3–9, they need to be replaced every 3 years or so to maintain vitality.

Artemisia (*wormwood*). Native to many parts of the world, with an ancient history as a medicinal, magical, and cooking herb, these perennials are valued more for their feathery aromatic leaves than for their inconspicuous white flowers.

Depending on the species, artemisias may grow as tall as the 4′ willowy 'Silver King' or be as low and cushion-like as the 8″ 'Silver Mound'. All are attractive foils for brighter, more floriferous plants. Artemisias generally grow rapidly in almost any soil, as long as it drains well, but prefer dry sandy soil to rich loam, in full sun or light shade. They need frequent division and the climatic conditions of zones 4 or 5 to 8 or 9, depending on the species.

Aster (*Michaelmas daisy*). Perennial asters, once rather disease-prone, are now available in resistant hybrid species that can be counted on as beautiful performers, especially in the late-summer and fall garden. The predominant colors of the aster family are lavender and blue, sometimes with contrasting yellow centers. Newer species include many other colors such as the New England asters 'Harrington's Pink' and 'September Ruby', with profusions of pink and cerise flowers on 4'–5' plants. Asters also offer a considerable range in size, from low-growing *A. asteroides*, only 6" tall, to some New York asters that stand 5'–6' tall at maturity. All asters grow well in full sun and well-drained soil, and taller species benefit from having canes pinched back to encourage more flowering and stronger stems. Zones 4–9 are congenial for most asters.

Astilbe. The tiny individual flowers cluster as fluffy plumes of white, pink, lavender, or red on erect or arching stems, with lush, fresh-looking, fernlike leaves, deep green to bronze in color. Most astilbe cultivars grow 18"–24" tall, are mound-shaped in habit, and flower in June and July. They rank as long-lived performers suitable especially for areas of light shade. They are profligate feeders that will always benefit from annual feeding, plenty of moisture, a soil supplemented with leaf mold or peat moss, and division every 2–3 years. They are hardy in zones 4–8, though some winter protection is advised in colder areas.

Aubrieta (*rock cress*). A longtime favorite of traditional garden beds, especially in its variegated foliage forms, rock cress appears today most often in modern hybrid mixtures whose diminutive 2"–8" heights make them especially suitable for rock gardens, walls, and the fronts of borders. Rock cresses bloom in April and May in deep shades of pink,

rose, and purple, and with their thrifty, dense foliage look especially handsome when interplanted with spring bulbs. Culture requirements include well-drained soil, plenty of sun, and a climate range of zones 4–8.

A close relative is the genus *Arabis* (wall rock cress), which is distinguished chiefly by its grey-green leaves.

Aurinia saxatilis (*basket-of-gold*). Basket-of-gold is a low-growing perennial with small, elongated grey-green leaves and tiny bright lemon-yellow flowers that are very colorful in their massy profusion in April and May. A favorite for rock gardens, its habit is somewhat variable depending upon soil conditions, from compact in dry, poor soil to open and loose in rich, moist soil. Basket-of-gold should be cut back after flowering, to keep it vigorous. The species likes full sun and dry, poor, infertile soil, which makes it a true friend of gardeners who must work in difficult conditions. It is hardy to zone 3.

Campanula (*bellflower*). Ranked among the most versatile of border flowers, there is a bellflower for almost any garden location and situation. For example, *C. carpatica*, the Carpathian harebell, forms small, round, blue, violet, or white cup-shaped flowers from July to September, and at 6"–9" tall, is a fine selection for rock gardens and border edging. *C. lactiflora* offers 4'–5' tall branching heads of white to pale blue flowers and belongs somewhat farther back in a border arrangement. *C. poscharskyana* is distinguished for its delicate sprays of mauve-blue flowers and its trailing habit from early spring to late autumn. Campanulas like moderately fertile, moist, well-drained soil in full to partial sun, zones 4–8.

Centaurea montana (*mountain bluet*). Large, elegant, thistle-shaped fringed flowers in a rich cornflower blue appear for six weeks in

May and June, then rebloom sporadically in late summer if dead-headed. Plants grow to about 2' in height and sport silvery-grey foliage. Centaureas favor well-drained soil and a sunny location in zones 4–8.

Chrysanthemum. The garden mum comes in an amazing range of heights (6" to 6'), in myriad growth forms (dwarf, slender upright, bushy, and cascading), in numerous flower forms (pompom, spider, daisy, spoon), and in virtually every color but blue. Most start blooming in late summer and continue to delight through early frosts. All chrysanthemums benefit from pinching back and moderately fertile, moist soil. In colder areas, plants need some winter protection, such as a deep covering of evergreen boughs or salt hay after the ground has frozen, though many gardeners prefer to dig them up and keep them in a cold frame over the winter. Some favorite chrysanthemums are *C. parthenium,* feverfew, which presents 1'–2' mounds of tiny daisylike white flowers, good for edgings; *C. Weyrichii,* with its masses of single white daisies 12" above shiny green foliage, good in rock gardens; and *C. × superbum* (alternately *C. maximum*), the shasta daisy, always white, in single or double varieties, in heights to 4' and with a blooming pattern that begins in July. (A standout in any garden, the shasta daisy is one of the few Victorian chrysanthemums still around, and is the species of choice for old-fashioned gardens.) Chrysanthemums are generally hardy in zones 4–9.

Clematis. Masses of showy flowers in shades of white, pink, maroon, blue, and purple are produced on vines, some climbing and others that need tying or staking. For best effect train the woody sort on an arbor or use them against a wall or fence at the back of a bed. One of the most popular varieties is *C.* 'Nelly Moser'. The 7"–9" flowers, their pale pink petals cen-ter-striped with a deeper pink, appear profusely in May and June and again in September. *C. × jackmanii,* with large deep purple blossoms, is the best-known clematis. Most clematis grow well in full sun or light shade, slightly acid to neutral soil, and are hardy in zones 4–8.

Clematis patens *'Nelly Moser'*

Coreopsis. These summer bloomers are reliable yellow-flowering perennials that can be selected to bloom from early summer (*C. verticillata*) to late summer and early fall (*C. tinctoria*). They also offer a range of leaf forms, with most having broad leaves but *C. verticillata* having elegant, dark green ferny foliage. Coreopsis are typically sun loving, easy to grow, and hardy to zone 3.

Delphinium. Delphiniums are a challenge to grow, as they are subject to garden slugs and fungi, often require staking, and are somewhat choosy about soil conditions, but their magnificent blue flower spikes, which appear in June and July, earn the gardener's forgiveness. Delphiniums prefer cool summer climates, full sun, a slightly alkaline soil, and rotted manure, or some other sort of well-balanced feeding, annually. Still, they peter out after three or four seasons and need to be replaced. Depending upon variety, they are hardy as far north as zone 3; south to zone 8.

Dianthus *(pink).* Pinks are valued both for their neat mounds of silver and green foliage and for their abundant displays of fragrant pink, red, and white carnation-shaped miniature flowers, which appear in June. Pinks are typically ground-covering plants and good front-row performers. Old-fashioned pinks, known as Sweet William or *D. barbatus*, are a tender perennial best treated as a biennial and planted in drifts. Dianthus like full sun and climatic conditions found in zones 4–8, with some varieties being more restricted.

Dicentra *(bleeding heart).* This romantic spring bloomer with pendant heart-shaped flowers on delicately fringed green leaves is one of the worthiest of garden plants, meriting the extra degree of attention it sometimes needs. The species *D. spectabilis* is distinguished for its arching wands of long-lived pink or white hearts. It is especially suitable for old-fashioned Victorian gardens, in full sun or partial shade and moist to somewhat dry soil, in zones 3–9.

Digitalis *(foxglove).* Both Latin and English names refer to the finger- or tubular-shaped flowers of this woodland plant, which has been developed in recent years to offer a multitude of heights and colors. *D. grandiflora* is one of the few true perennials and bears yellow flowers on 3' stalks. *D. purpurea* or purple foxglove is a biennial, with pink or white flowers that bloom in early to midsummer, and grows to a height of 6'. The 'Excelsior' hybrids, truly extraordinary plants in many ways, have atypical horizontal flowers in white, cream, pink, maroon, red, peach, and yellow that reach 8' under good conditions. All foxgloves like well-drained soil, partial shade, and are hardy in zones 4–8.

Echinops *(globe thistle).* The large, bold, almost spherical blue flower of the globe thistle appears in late summer and provides a useful contrast in form in a mixed border. Its rather unattractive spiny stems and foliage are best hidden behind some other greenery, so many gardeners prefer to plant this tallish perennial in a middle-of-the-border location where only its best feature shows. Echinops grows in full sun or partial shade, in average well-drained soil, and sets dense roots about 1' deep, which makes the necessary periodic division rather difficult. It is hardy to zone 3.

Eranthis *(winter aconite).* One of the most rewarding of the spring-flowering plants, even earlier in its appearance than the crocus, this tuberous perennial thrusts buttercup-like yellow flowers above frilly ruffs of ground-hugging green leaves even as the snow is melting. They look particularly pleasing when planted with an intermix of white snowdrops (*Galanthus*) and will naturalize rather quickly if left alone in a corner of a rock garden. Or, as they are very inexpensive, you can mass them from the start. They are hardy in zones 4–9.

Euphorbia *(spurge).* Euphorbias have petal-like leaves or bracts that in their handsome arrangement appear to be flowers; their true flowers, which develop in the center of the bracts, come and go in early to midsummer, but the bracts keep spurge attractive through most of the growing season. *E. epithymoides*, cushion spurge, grows a foot tall and attains a width of 2′; its bracts are bright yellow in spring and early summer, reddish in fall. *E. corollata*, flowering spurge, grows considerably taller and produces minute white bracts. *E. griffithii* has orange-scarlet bracts and grows to 30″ tall. Euphorbias are drought-resistant plants that need full sun and well-drained soil. Depending on the species, they grow in zones 3–10.

Gaillardia *(blanket flower)*. Bright daisy-type flame red, orange, or red flowers have a blooming season that extends from June to August if dead-headed regularly. Foliage grows in tidy mounds that range in height from 8″ to 3′, the larger sorts requiring staking. Noted for their ease of care, gaillardias are largely pest-free, heat and drought resistant, and flourish in zones 3–9. Blanket flowers also make excellent cut flowers.

Geranium *(hardy geraniums, as distinguished from the common garden geraniums of the genus* Pelargonium*)*. Hardy geraniums grow in nicely rounded, compact mounds of fresh green lobed leaves that, depending upon the species' size, can be used as a ground cover to middle-of-border plants. Most hardy geraniums bear flowers in the pink-crimson-purple-lavender range, atop stems that rise as much as 8″ above their foliage; they bloom

Euphorbia griffithii 'Fireglow'

from late spring to August. Most are vigorous and easy to grow in sun or partial shade, so long as the soil has enough humus content to maintain a reasonable level of moisture. They are generally hardy in zones 4–8.

Geum. Geums are generally brilliantly colored orange to scarlet flowering perennials. They bear open-faced inch-wide single or double blossoms from May to August if deadheaded. And they hover 24″–30″ above dense basal clumps of large deep green leaves. Older varieties, such as 'Mrs. Bradshaw', require division every other year, but newer hybrids can often go for several years without attention. Geums perform best in full sun, a well-drained soil with plenty of organic material, and they are hardy to zone 5.

Geranium

Gypsophila (baby's breath). A familiar part of floral bouquets, the feathery sprays of tiny double white flowers that distinguish gypsophila make this perennial equally valuable in old-fashioned beds and borders. The most popular form of baby's breath nowadays is 'Bristol Fairy', which grows to 3′ and flowers all summer long. Once the plant gets established and is growing vigorously, its branches should be firmly caged with stakes and strings for support. Gypsophila needs full sun, a well-drained, slightly alkaline soil which probably means a lime dressing every 2–3 years, and sufficient depth to accommodate its taproot. It is hardy in zones 3–9.

Heliopsis (false sunflower, oxeye). A robust, almost coarse-looking flower that looks a little like a small sunflower, this perennial seems most at home in an informal border, especially when paired with red or deep pink daylilies. It flowers from July until frost and fares better than most perennials in dry soils. Some species grow to 5′ tall and all are hardy in zones 4–9.

Hemerocallis (daylily). Among the most resilient flowering plants known, daylilies have been bred and developed to an extraordinary degree so that today the offerings available to the amateur gardener number in the hundreds. Basically trumpet-shaped, they come with smooth and ruffled petals, in countless single or bi-colors. Their long-bladed, arching foliage also varies in color and size. Though each flower blooms for just one day, they produce great numbers of flowers in sequence, so that each plant ends up looking attractive for several weeks; by careful staging and the right selections, the gardener can design a bed that is flowering with nothing but daylilies from July through September. Daylilies typically multiply quickly by their underground rhizomes, and if given the chance will soon weave such a dense presence that competing weeds are driven out, making hemerocallis one of the best choices for a low-maintenance garden. They like good garden soil, plenty of sun for maximum flowering, and are generally hardy in zones 4–9.

Hosta (plantain lily). Hostas win friends through their gorgeous foliage and are only secondarily appreciated for their little lavender or white bell-shaped flowers, which appear in midsummer. Hosta's leaves rise from a central crown, are broad and shiny, and, depending upon the particular selection, may be streaked, puckered, wavy-edged, dramatically veined, and in shades of green, grey, or slate blue. Their rounded forms, 8″–30″ tall, make them excellent choices as specimen plants or, massed, as ground cover. Hostas like rich, moist, well-drained soil, and prosper in light to medium shade in zones 3–9.

Iris germanica (bearded iris, German iris). There is hardly a part of the world that has not contributed some piece to the huge mosaic that constitutes the modern 150-member iris genus. Probably the best known, however, is the "bearded" iris species that blooms in late spring. This species takes its popular name from the three flower petals that hang down, beardlike, below the three "standard" upright petals. Bearded iris vary considerably in height—some dwarf varieties being as little as 4″ tall, some giant varieties growing to a splendid 4′. Foliage consists of sword-shaped grey-green blades that are stiffly erect. Tall stems bearing the flowers on pedicels arise from the foliage. Flower colors and color combinations vary widely. Bearded iris like a neutral, well-drained soil in full sun or partial shade in zones 4–8.

Iris kaempferi (Japanese iris). A larger, more massive species of iris, the Japanese plants

Iris sibirica *'Harpswell Haze'*

produce huge, flat "beardless" blossoms in a range of blue, lavender, pink, and purple above dark green bladed foliage. Some plants reach an overall height of 6′. They need acid soil and are unusual in tolerating boggy soil such as is found on pond banks. They are happy in sun or partial shade and hardy to zone 4.

Iris sibirica (Siberian iris). Siberian iris, which bear dainty blossoms in June and July, have uncommonly narrow, slightly arching leaves. Depending upon variety, they range in size from 18″ to 36″ in shades of white, blue, and purple. Easy to care for, the Siberians are not too fussy about soil so long as it is slightly acid. They flower best in full sun, though they tolerate partial shade. Thanks to their origins, the species is hardy to zone 3.

Iris versicolor (blue flag). Blue flag is native to the American wetlands. It grows to 3' and is ideal for pond and stream margins and other boggy areas, so long as it gets full sun. The species is hardy in zones 4–8.

Lamium maculatum (dead nettle). This member of the mint family makes a bright and beautiful low-maintenance ground cover. Some varieties offer unusual silver leaves, and small spikes of white, pink, or purple flowers bloom from late spring through summer. Lamiums thrive in average soil and partial shade, and are generally hardy in zones 4–9.

Lavandula (lavender). With over 20 species of lavender available, only a few are perennial in most of the U.S. English lavender (*L. officinalis*, alternately *L. angustifolia* or *L. vera*) is a wonderful exception. English lavender is a bushy perennial that grows to 3' and covers itself with glorious spikes of aromatic lavender-colored flowers in summer. 'Hidcote Blue' is a modern cultivar, the deepest blue of several offerings, that grows to about 2' and makes a compact, low, and fragrant hedge. English lavenders like full sun, well-drained soil, and are hardy in zones 5–9.

Lilium (lily). This outstanding genus of bulbs is indigenous to the northern temperate zone and, thanks to extensive breeding improvements in recent decades, comes in so many fine, disease-resistant hybrids that a gardener in many parts of the U.S. can specialize in lilies and have a sequence of colorful bloomers from late May through September. Flowers vary from trumpet shape, the old standbys, to exotic open forms that resemble dahlias, and from the very large to the dainty. And in terms of color selection, only blue is lacking from the lily palette. Lilies like to have "their heads warm and their feet cool," as the old saying goes, so they are best planted where they will receive filtered sunlight and

nestle in an over-planting of low-growing perennials or annuals that shade the earth. Taller hybrids may need staking. Some species are hardy as far north as zone 4 or 5, others only to zone 7, so check before you order your bulbs.

Liriope (lilyturf). Liriopes are particularly favored in the South and Southwest, where their clumping forms and evergreen grass-like leaves make them a standout ground cover. In addition, lilyturf species also bear tiny ¼-inch lavender, blue, or white flowers on spikes from midsummer to fall, followed by decorative blue-black berries. Lilyturfs do well in almost any soil, will tolerate a wide range of light conditions, and are hardy at least to zone 6, with the creeper, *L. spicata*, resistant to zone 5.

Lupinus (lupine). Long, show-off spikes of flowers thrust upward from handsome palmate foliage from midspring to midsummer. Descendants of native lupines such as the Texas bluebonnet, the modern 'Russell Hybrids' are the principal varieties sold in nurseries today. They come in blue, rose, lavender, yellow, salmon, purple, and many bicolors, and in heights ranging from a compact 2' to a tall back-of-border 4'. Lupines favor deep, moist, acid soil, a deep mulch, and are hardy in zones 4–7. Relatively short-lived as perennials go, lupines can sometimes be made to self-sow.

Lysimachia punctata (yellow loosestrife). A tough, carefree perennial that grows in sun or partial shade, this plant sends up graceful, arching spikes of small yellow flowers in abundance from late spring through summer. It grows 2½'–3' tall, needs no staking, but tends to be invasive except when planted alongside equally vigorous growers like daylilies. This loosestrife is hardy to zone 4.

Lilium 'Headlight'

Lythrum salicaria *(purple loosestrife)*. These flowering giants grow in any sunny location that is not too dry. Various cultivars produce pink, crimson, or magenta spires, 3'–6' high, from late June to September. Choose a variety that is specifically sterile to avoid having your bed overrun. Hardy in zones 3–9.

Monarda didyma *(bee balm)*. The strong upright stems of this perennial bear dark green, mintlike aromatic leaves and bright, fluffy bursts of flower petals. They are available in scarlet, pink, white, and light purple, with the scarlets being notably attractive to hummingbirds. Rapid spreaders, they are best di-

vided every 3–4 years to maintain vigor. Most grow to a height of 2'–3', making them good middle-of-the-border selections in sun and partial shade locations. Hardy to zone 4.

Narcissus *(daffodil)*. The genus *Narcissus* contains about 26 species, divided according to their unique combinations of characteristics. Most of us know them as daffodils, jonquils, paper whites, and polyanthus narcissus, without being sure which is which. All of them are notably easy to grow, tolerant of light shade as well as full sun, and many are given to naturalizing or multiplying wherever they are planted. First in consideration and first in April come the wild or species daffodils, typically rather small, fragrant, and uniformly golden in color. These with their tiny size belong in a rock garden. Following the wild daffodils come the hybrids. These include *N. cyclamineus*, an early white and yellow bloomer, 6"–10" tall; modern Flatcup or Weatherproof narcissus, noted for large, flat, often bicolored flowers, vigorous sturdy stems, and late April bloom; Trumpets, with deeper cups and greater heights than other species; and jonquils, of outstanding fragrance. Hardiness varies considerably, so check before you order bulbs.

Oenothera (evening primrose). Although called evening primrose, these plants are actually afternoon bloomers, producing sunny yellow flowers that look rather like oversized, open buttercups from early summer onwards. Varieties range in height from 12" to 2' tall. Leaves are long, slender, green to reddish brown. They grow in zones 4–9 in full sun and well-drained soil.

Paeonia (peony). A shrublike perennial of astonishingly long life, the hybrid peony comes in many floral shapes, colors, and sizes, and is considered by many gardeners to be a mainstay in the perennial border because of its gorgeous, fragrant flowers, its neat, bushy 3'-high form, and its handsome green foliage, which remains in good order until frost. Peonies typically bloom in May and June, and depending upon the hybrid, may produce flowers in shades of rosy red, pink, white, or yellow, in single, double, semidouble, Japanese, or anemone form. Peonies require full sun, a deep rich soil for best results, and are hardy to zone 5.

Papaver orientale (Oriental poppy). The poppy flower is so showy during its short life (a couple of weeks in late spring to early summer) that many gardeners are more than willing to tuck a few in among later-blooming plants just to see them return each year. Poppy blooms range from traditional scarlet-orange to newer pinks, reds, oranges, and whites, 4"–10" across, on curvaceous stems that can reach 4' heights. Poppies require full sun to partial shade, well-drained soil, and are hardy to zone 3.

Phlox paniculata (garden phlox). A direct descendant of the wild North American native, the garden phlox is the backbone of many a summer border, blooming from July through August on plants that grow 3'–4' tall. Flowers, which cluster rather like lilac blossoms, range from crimson and scarlet to pink, purple, and white; foliage is dark green and modestly attractive. Summer phlox like full sun or light shade and a moist rich soil, and are hardy in zones 4–9.

Phlox subulata (moss phlox). Among the standout perennials for border edgings and rock gardens, moss phlox are distinguished by their mass of narrow, spinelike evergreen leaves that are actually soft to the touch, and abundant flowers that range in color from pinks and lavenders to white. Moss phlox flowers for 3–4 weeks in late spring, and as lateral shoots fan out from the center stock the plant sets down additional roots, soon filling in to create pretty drifts that will cascade over walls if permitted. The species requires full sun and good drainage in zones 3–9.

Potentilla (cinquefoil). These perennials are typically low-growing, with bright five-petaled blooms like small single roses in colors from crimson red to white, and attractive dark green foliage that makes them a good choice for front-of-border or rock garden display. Potentillas bloom from June to frost and like plenty of sun, well-drained soil, and the climate of zones 4–8.

Primula (*primrose*). A huge and complex genus of flowering perennials, the primulas vary in height from a few inches tall to as much as 3'. Old-fashioned gardens welcome the *P. vulgaris*, which is a close cousin of the wild primrose; and dusky-colored cultivars of *P. auricula* are apt choices for a Victorian garden. Primroses look their best when planted in drifts and are spring bloomers in the North, winter bloomers in the South and Pacific Southwest. In the moist, acid soil and half-shade they favor they will often seed prolifically. Hardy in zones 5–9, depending upon the species.

Rudbeckia fulgida **'Goldsturm'** (*black-eyed Susan*). Much appreciated for its long flowering season, this improved cultivar of the wild black-eyed Susan blooms from midsummer until frost. Its daisy flowers are a rich golden yellow with dark brown centers. Plants grow to about 2 feet tall; other varieties grow taller and may require staking. Rudbeckias like full sun but will tolerate light shade as long as they stand in well-drained soil in zones 3–9.

Salvia (*sage*). Salvia is a handsome foliage plant that takes many forms. *S. Sclarea* is a stately 3'-tall herb that bears whorls of whitish flowers tinged with purple, above large, velvety, oval leaves. *S. blancoana* is a low, spreading bush with narrow silver-grey leaves tipped with soft blue flowers in midsummer. *S. argentea* or silver sage has large, oval, woolly leaves that look like spun silver. *S. officinalis* is the fabled herb of the ancients, which comes in various green, golden, and purple varieties. *S. haematodes* or bloodvein sage grows 2'–3' tall, and sends up tiny ½" violet flower spikes from neat rosettes of grey-green leaves in early to midsummer. All perennial sages prefer full sun and well-drained, light soil. Most are hardy in zones 4–9, though *S. officinalis* is slightly more rugged and silver sage

Salvia Sclarea *'Alba'*

is probably too tender for anything north of zone 5.

Santolina (*lavender cotton*). Valued for its silvery grey fernlike foliage, lavender cotton is generally kept compact through shearing, with the result that its tiny, buttonlike yellow flowers seldom have a chance to set. Lavender cotton is often used in mass plantings along the forward edge of a border, especially in zones 6–9 where it is a perennial, though it can also be planted as an annual farther north. Santolina needs full sun but it is not choosy about soil.

Sedum (*stonecrop*). One of the most versatile of the succulents, stonecrops have thick, fleshy light green leaves that cluster in neatly

Tulipa

rounded mounds and store water through dry spells. Many stonecrops grow close to the ground, which makes them good rock garden plants. The great new cultivar 'Autum Joy' has flat heads of tiny flowers, which resemble broccoli florets in size and form, and starts blooming in August, in colors ranging from pink and rose to white; they turn a deep bronze just before frost. It grows to 2'. Drought tolerant, happy in full sun or light shade and in almost any soil, the stonecrops are hardy to zone 3.

Stachys byzantina (lamb's ears). Attractive, woolly-textured, tongue-shaped silver leaves below 12"–18" tall flowering stalks with pinkish-purple flowers in June. (For gardeners who want to emphasize the foliage, flowers may be trimmed away.) *S. grandiflora*, the popular big betony, has distinctly different, deeply veined and wrinkled heart-shaped leaves and sets whorls of bright purple flowers in early to mid summer; the plants are also somewhat larger than lamb's ears, rising to 3' at maturity. Both species do best in full sun and well-drained soil, need dividing every 2–3 years, and grow in zones 4–9.

Tulipa (tulip). Tulips exist in innumerable varieties, thanks to the earnest efforts of breeders over the last several hundred years. There are colors, shapes, textures, heights, and flowering times to suit almost every gardener's needs. Indeed, if it were not for the fact that tulips tend to look rather messy in the garden after they have bloomed, they would be *the* perfect flowering plant for the first half of the gardening year; as it is, tulips need to be planted where their spent foliage can be hidden behind and under other plants in June. Wild tulips or botanical species tulips are, generally speaking, the smallest and earliest of the genus, and they have the distinct advantage of being reliably perennial, lasting up to 20 years in favorable sites. They come in heights of 3″–12″ in colors of cream, yellow, and red, crave sun, and look very much at home in the foreground of a rock garden. The early species tulips are followed by hybrids and cultivars, and while it is difficult to summarize them in any altogether useful way, it can generally be said that the "earlies" start flowering in April, followed by some of the Kaufmannianas, Fosterianas, and Darwins in May. These plus the Greigii and Lily-flowered tulips can be counted on for midseason display. And late flowering, which is to say late May and even early June in some areas, is also carried on by Darwin hybrids and Parrot tulips. Depending upon the specific selection and site, the hybrids may grow anywhere from 14″ to 30″ tall, and many will expend themselves within a couple of years and need replacing. All require full sun and a hardiness zone somewhere between 4 and 8.

Veronica (speedwell). Veronicas are highly valued as long-blooming plants that grow 12″–48″ tall and bear colorful spikes of tiny flowers that are typically blue, but sometimes lavender, pink, or white. Depending on their variety, their bloom period can be anywhere from early to late summer, with many producing throughout the entire season. They need full sun and well-drained soil, periodic division, and a climate zone from 4–8.

Author's Acknowledgments

I would like to thank Marta Hallett and Ellen Milionis at Running Heads for making this project a reality. Thanks are also due to Charles de Kay of Running Heads, a sterling editor, to Frances Tenenbaum of Houghton Mifflin for her support, and to Kathleen Nelson at Nelson Perennials in South Kent, Connecticut.

Photographers' Acknowledgments

*T*o photograph a gardening book successfully requires the assistance of many people. The photographers would like to thank the following people and organizations without whose help this book could not have come into being:

Marty Adams
Barbara Ashmun
Randy Baldwin
    of San Marcos Growers
Geoffrey Beasley
Loie Benedict
Kurt Bluemel
Joel and Joan Brink
Caprilands Herb Farm
Anne Carr
Charles Cresson
Hugh Dargan
Mary Palmer Dargan
Eve Davis
Charles de Kay
Mary Rose Duffield
Susan Dulaney
Dumbarton Oaks
Yvonne England
    of England's Herb Farm
Linda Engstrom
Ginger Epstein

Dan Franklin
Frances Franklin
Pam Frost
Ryan Gainey
Mrs. Gaiser
Mike and Helen Greenburg
Harland Hand
Connie Hansen
Virginia Hays and
    Stephanie Schutley
    of Santa Barbara
    Water Gardens
Alex Hill
Franziska Reed Huxley
Longwood Gardens
Pam Lord
Jan McDougal
Ann McPhail
Ildo Marra
Steve Martino
Meadowbrook Farm

Wolfgang Oehme and
    Jim van Sweden
Vera Peck
Roger Post
Paul and Barb Rawlings
Joanna Reed
Jan and Alan Rose
Joo and Gloria Sacco
Michael Schultz
Carol Shuler
Bill Smith
Mary Smith
The Sundial Herb Farm
John and Ann Swan
Sir John Thuron
Will Venard and Jan Wathen
Karen Weaver
Jim and Betty Weht
Cynthia White
Rick William
Tom Woodham
Chris Woods of Chanticleer

INDEX

Page numbers in italic indicate illustrations.

A

acanthus, *124*
Achillea (yarrow), *75*, 140
Achillea 'Moonshine', *49*
aconites, *51*
Aconitum (monkshood), 140
agaves, *136*
ageratums, 131
Alberta spruce, 17
Alchemilla (lady's mantle), *58*, 82, *102*, *117*, 140
Allium (ornamental onion), 140
alpine, 84, *84*, 88, *89*, 124
alyssum, *42*, 67
American Rock Garden Society, 89
anemone, *130*
Anemone blanda (windflower), 116, 140
Anemone x *hybrida* (Japanese anemone), 140
Anemone pulsatilla (pasqueflower), 141
Anthemis tinctoria (golden marguerite), 141
aquatic grasses, 74
Aquilegia (columbine), 112, 141
Arrhenatherum bulbosum, *114*
Artemisia (wormwood), *93*, *102*, 112, 141
Aster (Michaelmas daisy), 112, 142
astilbe, *124*, 142
Aubrieta (rock cress), *43*, 142
Aurinia saxatilis (basket-of-gold), 88, *117*, *126*, 142
azalea, *18*, *24*, *32*, *44*, *101*, *106*, 116

B

baby's breath (*Gypsophila*), 146
basil, *79*
basket-of-gold (*Aurinia saxatilis*), 88, *117*, *126*, 142
bearded iris (*Iris germanica*), 147
bee balm (*Monarda didyma*), 149
bellflower (*Campanula*), 99, 112, 142
bergenia, *58*, *102*
'Betty Prior' floribunda, *69*
birdbath, *106*
black-eyed Susan (*Rudbeckia fulgida* 'Goldsturm'), 151
blanket flower (*Gaillardia*), 99, 145
bleeding heart (*Dicentra*), 144
blueberries, 78
blue flag (*Iris versicolor*), 148
blue oat grass (*Helictotrichon sempervirens*), *27*
bog plants, 74
bougainvillea, *137*
boxwood, *35*, 56, *102*, *130*, 131
brittlebush, 136
Brown, Lancelot "Capability," 57
bugbane, *20*
bush sage (*Salvia Greggii*), 136

C

cabbage, 78
cactus, *39*, *84*, *88*, *135*, *136*, *137*
calceolaria, *18*
calendula, 79
camellia, 102
campanula (bellflower), 99, 112, 142
candytuft, 80, *128*
cannas, *30*
cardoon, 102
carnation (*Dianthus*), *50*, *51*, 112
Carolina lupine, *99*
carpet-bedding, 57
celosia, 131
centaurea, 67
Centaurea montana (mountain bluet), 142
centerpieces, 106–109
China-asters, 131–132
chrysanthemum, 143
'Chrysler Imperial' hybrid tea roses, *69*
cinquefoil (*Potentilla*), 150
clematis, *96*, 143
climbing hydrangea (*Hydrangea petiolaris*), 82
color scheming, 44–47
color strategy, 48–49
columbine (*Aquilegia*), 112, 141
columbine meadow rue, *28*
common speedwell, *90*
coneflowers, 80
coral bells, *99*
Coreopsis, *51*, 143

Cotinus coggyria (smoke tree), *117*
cotoneaster, 102
cottage pinks (*Dianthus*), *25*, *99*
cranes bill, *98*
crassula, *136*
creeping juniper, 88
crocus, 88

D

daffodil (*Narcissus*), 42, 149
daisy, *20*, *47*
daisy bush, 102
'Dark Delight' New Zealand flax (*Phormium*), *27*
daylily (*Hemerocallis*), 79, *99*, 112, 146
dead nettle (*Lamium maculatum*), 80, *98*, 148
delphinium, *51*, 112, 144
desert marigold, *135*, 137
Dianthus (pink), 144
Dicentra (bleeding heart), 144
Digitalis (foxglove), *89*, *99*, *110*, 112, 116, 144
dwarf dahlia, 132
dwarf evergreen, 84, 88
dwarf Japanese barberry 'Crimson Pygmy', *106*
dwarf rhododendron, 88

E

Echinops (globe thistle), *22*, 93, 144
edgings, 40–41
eggplant, 78
elecampane (*Inula Helenium*), *86*
English primrose, *98*
English ivy (*Hedera helix*), *131*
Eranthis (winter aconite), 144
Eschscholzia Californica (California poppy), *20*, *126*, 137
Euonymus microphylla, *71*
euphorbia (spurge), 88, *126*, 144
evening primrose (*Oenothera*), 150

F

false sunflower (*Heliopsis*), 146
fatsia, 102
fern, *18*, 84, 102
fertilizer, 27, 29
feverfew (*Chrysanthemum parthenium*), *93*
firecracker, 136
flax, 102
forget-me-not, *16*, *43*
forsythia, 112
fountain grass, 80
fountains, *108*
foxglove (*Digitalis*), 89, *99*, 110, 112, 116, 144
fritillaria, 42

G

Gaillardia (blanket flower), *99*, 145
garden phlox (*Phlox paniculata*), 150
garden styles,
    by the water, 72–75
    dry garden, 134–137
    edible beds, 76–79
    formal, 35–37, 41, 54–55, 60, 63, 68, 74, *107*, 130–133
    green gardens, 100–105
    herbal gardens, 90–93
    in the city, 80–83
    informal, 38–39, 41
    old-fashioned beds, 110–113
    rock gardens, 84–89
    wild gardens, 94–99
    woodland gardens, 114–117
gazania, 132
gentian (*Gentiana*), 88
geranium (*Pelargonium*), *49*, *101*, *106*, 132
German iris (*Iris germanica*), 147
germander, 56, 131
Geum, 146
globe thistle (*Echinops*), 22, 93, 144

goatsbeard, *58*
golden marguerite (*Anthemis tinctoria*), 141
Gumpo azalea, *101*, *106*
gunnera, 102
Gypsophila (baby's breath), 146

H

hardy geranium, 117, 145
harebell (*Campanula alpina*), 88
Hedera helix (English ivy), *131*
Helictotrichon sempervirens (blue oat grass), 27
Heliopsis (false sunflower, oxeye), 146
heliotrope, *31*, *73*, 132
hellebore, 102
Hemerocallis (daylily), 79, *99*, 112, 146
Himalayan primrose (*Primula denticulata*), *12*
history of gardening, 56–57, 76, 90, 106
holly, 102, *130*
hollyhocks, 112
hop bush, 136
Hosta (plantain lily), *28*, 80, *98*, *101*, *105*, 147

I

'Iceberg' floribunda, *69*
Iceland poppy, *26*
Ilex, *102*
impatiens, 82, 132
Inula Helenium (elecampane), *86*
iris, *18*, *47*, 110, 112, 116, 147, 148
Iris germanica (bearded iris, German iris), 147
Iris kaempferi (Japanese iris), 147
Iris sibirica (Siberian iris), *18*, 110, 147
Iris versicolor (blue flag), 148
ivy (*Hedera*), *82*, *131*, *132*

J

Jacob's ladder, *117*
Japanese anemone (*Anemone* x *hybrida*), 140
Japanese iris (*Iris kaempferi*), 147
Japanese maple, *16*
Jekyll, Gertrude, 9, 49, 57, 67, 68
jojoba, 136

K

kale, 78

L

lady's mantle (*Alchemilla*), *58*, 82, *102*, *117*, 140
lady's slipper, 116
lamb's ears (*Stachys byzantina*), 49, 93, 102, 152
Lamium maculatum (dead nettle), 80, 98, 148
lantana, 132
lavender (*Lavandula*), *51*, 93, 102, 131, 148
lavender cotton (*Santolina*), *90*, 93, *93*, 102, *106*, 151
Le Nôtré, André, 55
lettuce, *77*, 78, *78*
lilac, 47, 112
lily (*Lilium*), 47, 116, 148
Liriope (lilyturf), 148
lobelia, *31*, *58*, 132
lotus, 74
lupine, 112, 148
Lysimachia punctata (yellow loosestrife), 46, 149
Lythrum salicaria (purple loosestrife), 112, 149

M

maiden grass, 80
maintaining a garden, 29, 52–53, 93, 132
mallow, *75*
Maltese cross (*Lychnis chalcedonica*), *50*
mammillaria, 136
marigold, *30*, *67*, 132, *135*, 137
Meadowbrook Farm, *74*
mesquite, *137*
Michaelmas daisy (*Aster*), 112, 142
Monarda didyma (bee balm), 149
Mondo grass (*Ophiopogon japonicus*), *101*
monkshood (*Aconitum*), 140
moss phlox (*Phlox subulata*), 150
mountain bluet (*Centaurea montana*), 142
mountain laurel, 116
mugo pine (*Pinus mugo*), 88

N

Narcissus (daffodil), 42, 149
nemesia, *126*
Nicolson, Harold, Sir, 47
nasturtium, 79

O

ocotillo, *137*
Oenothera (evening primrose), 150
okra, 78
Ophiopogon japonicus (Mondo grass), *101*
Opuntia (prickly pear), *39*, *84*, 88, *135*, 136, *137*
Oriental poppy (*Papaver orientale*), 150
ornamental cabbage, *77*
ornamental onion (*Allium*), 140
osmanthus, 102
oxeye (*Heliopsis*), 146

P

Paeonia (peony), 48, 150
pansy, *43*, *67*, *108*, *130*, *131*
Papaver orientale (Oriental poppy), 150
pasqueflower (*Pulsatilla patens*), 88
Pelargonium (geranium), *49*, *101*, *106*, 132
penstemons, 137
peony (*Paeonia*), 48, 112
peppers,
  bell, 78
  chili, *79*
Persian buttercups, *126*
Phlox paniculata (garden phlox), 150
Phlox subulata (moss phlox), 88, 116, 150
Phormium ('Dark Delight' New Zealand flax), *27*
planning a garden,
  aesthetics, 30–32
  best sites for, 24
  borders, 67–69
  by the water, 72–75
  centerpieces, 106–109
  color, 30–32, 44–49, 67, 68, 102, *105*
  edible beds, 76–79
  edging, 40–41
  fountains, 74
  in the city, 80–83
  lattices, 83
  layout, 24, 30–32, 35, 50–51, 58–65, 68, 72, 74, 83, 86, 90, 108, 130
  measuring for, 32, 37, 102, 110, 116, 131
  paths, 114, 130
  plant selection, 29, 30–32, 38, 41–49, 76–106, 110, 112, 116, 131, 132, 135–137
  raised beds and borders, 118–125
  shape and size, 30–32, 35, 37, 38, 50, 60–65, 120, 132
  soil conditions, 26–29, 80, 114–115, 118, 123, 135
  terraced beds, 126–129

vines, 82–83
walkways, 83
plantain lily (*Hosta*), *28*, *80*, *98*,
    101, *105*, 147
plumbago, *130*
poppy, *20*
    California poppy
        (*Eschscholzia Californica*),
        20, *126*, 137
    Iceland poppy, *26*
    Oriental poppy (*Papaver
        orientale*), 112, 150
portulaca, *136*
Potentilla (cinquefoil), 150
prickly pear (*Opuntia*), *39*, *84*,
    88, *135*, 136, *137*
primrose (*Primula*), 151
purple loosestrife (*Lythrum
    salicaria*), 112, 149

R

raised beds and borders, 118–
    125
ranunculus, *47*
rhododendron, 24, *32*, 116,
    117, *128*
rhubarb, 78, 102
Robinson, William, 22, 57
rock cress, *43*, 142
rockrose, *126*
Roman chamomile, *79*
rosemary, 131
roses, *47*, *69*, *96*, 112
Rudbeckia fulgida 'Goldsturm'
    (black-eyed Susan), 151

S

Sackville-West, Vita, 47
sage (*Salvia*), *75*, 112, 151
    bush sage (*Salvia Greggii*),
        136
sagebrush, 136
Salvia (sage), *75*, 112, 151
Santolina (lavender cotton), *90*,
    93, *93*, 102, *106*, 151
saxifrage, *105*
sculptures, 130
Sedum (stonecrop), *25*, 80, 88,
    136, 151
sempervivums, 88, *136*
senecio, 102

shooting star (*Podecatheon
    meadia*), 88
shortias, 24
Siberian iris (*Iris sibirica*), *18*,
    110, 147
silver sage, 93
silvery yarrow, 93
Sissinghurst Castle, 47
smoke tree, *117*
snakeroot, 116
snapdragons, *67*
speedwell (*Veronica*), *93*, 112,
    153
spurge (euphorbia), 88, *126*,
    144
Stachys byzantina (lamb's ears),
    49, *93*, 102, 152
statues as centerpieces, 106
stonecrop (*Sedum reflexum* and
    Sedum spurium), *25*, 151
strawberries, 78
succulents, 84
sundial, 106, *106*, 130, *131*
sundrops (*Oenothera tetragona*),
    22, 74
sweet alyssum, *67*

T

terraced beds, 126–129
thyme, *89*, *93*
tomatoes, 78, *79*
topsoil, 27
torenia, *130*
trailing arbutus, 116
trellis, 112, 130
trillium, 88, 116
tuberous begonias, *31*
tulip, *16*, *42*, *44*, *46*, 112, 153

V

valerian, *126*
verbena, *18*, *39*, *49*, 132, *135*
Veronica (speedwell), *93*, 112,
    153
Victorian-style bed, *43*

W

wallflower, *43*
waterlily, 74
wild dogwood, 116
windflower, 116, 140
winter aconite (*Eranthis*), 144
winter-creeper (*Euonymus
    fortunei*), 82
witch hazel, 116
woodland wildflower, 84, 88
woolly mint, 93
wormwood (*Artemisia*), *93*, 102,
    112, 141

X

Xeriscaping, 52, 58, 135, *135*,
    137

Y

yarrow (*Achillea filipendulina*),
    75, 140
yellow loosestrife (*Lysimachia
    punctata*), 46, 149
yucca, *42*, 102, 136

Z

zinnia, *67*, 132
zucchini, *79*